Facilitating groups

Jenny Rogers

 Open University Press

Open University Press
McGraw-Hill Education
McGraw-Hill House
Shoppenhangers Road
Maidenhead
Berkshire
England
SL6 2QL

email: enquiries@openup.co.uk
world wide web: www.openup.co.uk

and Two Penn Plaza, New York, NY 10121-2289, USA

Some material was previously published in *Facilitating Groups* by Jenny Rogers.
Copyright © Management Futures Ltd. 1999
This edition published 2010

A catalogue record of this book is available from the British Library

ISBN-13: 978-0-335-24096-8 (pb) 978-0-335-24097-5 (hb)
ISBN-10: 0-335-24096-8 (pb) 0-335-24097-6 (hb)

Library of Congress Cataloging-in-Publication Data
CIP data applied for

Typeset by RefineCatch Limited, Bungay, Suffolk
Printed in the UK by Bell and Bain Ltd., Glasgow

Fictitious names of companies, products, people, characters and/or data that may be
used herein (in case studies or in examples) are not intended to represent any real
individual, company, product or event.

Mixed Sources
Product group from well-managed
forests and other controlled sources
www.fsc.org Cert no. TT-COC-002769
© 1996 Forest Stewardship Council

FSC

The *McGraw·Hill* Companies

2002695
£19·99

For Charlie and Lucy

CENTRE	Lincoln
CHECKED	
ZONE	mauve
CLASS MARK / SUFFIX	658.402 ROG
LOAN PERIOD	1 month

Contents

Acknowledgements viii

Introduction 1

1 **What is facilitation?** 5

2 **The secret life of groups** 27

3 **Preparation and design** 55

4 **The room and other practicalities** 105

5 **Vital skills** 116

6 **Facilitator nightmares: what if . . .?** 138

7 **Wrapping it all up** 164

Bibliography 184

Index 187

Acknowledgements

My thanks to colleagues at Management Futures Ltd; all of them ace facilitators. I have learned so much from working with them. Thanks to Anne Brockbank, Lois Graessle and Leni Wildflower for their good ideas and friendship and to Wendi Dallanegra for organizing the Writing Shed – and for 30 years of friendship. Thanks also to Luke Rogers and Mary Beskin for their vital help with the diagrams, to Chris Radley for the cartoon in Chapter 1 (p. 9) and Steven Appleby and Lois Graessle for their kind permission to use the cartoons in Chapter 1 (p. 17), Chapter 4 (p. 110) and Chapter 6 (p. 155) from 'Meeting Together'.

I am always interested in readers' feedback. If you have comments on this book, please email me: Jenny@JennyRogersCoaching.com.

Introduction

The 'silly question' is the first intimation of some totally new development.
(*Alfred North Whitehead*)

If you wish to improve yourself, try silence or some other cleansing discipline that will gradually show you your true self.
(*The Tao of Leadership*, adapted by John Heider)

This book is for anyone who is or wants to be a facilitator. It is a book of practice and aimed at practitioners. It describes how to behave as a facilitator and how to deal with the many common challenges that this role presents. My assumption is that you may have a little but not much experience and that you are facing the task of facilitating with the mixture of excitement and dread that most of us bring to a demanding new task.

Facilitation is a broadly based skill. Here are some examples of the kinds of people who need it:

1   Professionals working in the fields of coaching, organizational consultancy and team coaching

   Rational thinking and traditional problem-solving are not what hold teams back, whereas emotion does and emotion is messy and unpredictable. That is why teams hire professional facilitators to run the off-site meetings now usually described as *awaydays*. It needs a neutral outsider to be able to see the patterns, challenge the entrenched beliefs and name the apparently unnameable.

2   Mediators

   Mediation is growing as a profession, much like its close cousin, coaching. Mediation is now required or offered as a standard part of much dispute resolution, ideally at the earliest possible stage, before a problem has grown to an expensive mess. In commercial disputes there may be many millions of pounds or dollars and dozens of fragile reputations at stake. At the other end of the spectrum is the pain of a married couple considering separation or divorce. Whenever mediation is needed emotion runs high. Anger, hurt, vengeance-seeking and despair are the norm. Mediators need to be able to work with this and facilitation is the prime tool they will use to do so.

3 Teachers and trainers in any setting, whether in secondary, further, higher or adult education

In all these fields, the days are long past when giving lectures is considered the default way to learn. As current research is showing so clearly, human adults learn best when our own ideas are solicited, challenged and supported. To do this you need to know how to facilitate. This has always been a feature of teaching and learning in the humanities but the facilitative approach has now spread to science. For instance, it is essential to use facilitation in the problem-based learning now so common in the newer medical schools across the world. As medical knowledge has expanded, it has become impossible to teach the curriculum in a lecture style – there is simply too much information to convey in the time available. In problem-based learning, students are presented with a provocatively ragged and incomplete case. The method is designed to teach problem-solving and diagnostic skills and to demonstrate a systemic and holistic approach to medicine. The students investigate and research and then meet with their tutor whose role is to facilitate the discussion rather than to pass on knowledge.

4 Anyone needing to know how to run a meeting where the aim is to encourage participation, energy, debate and commitment

When in this role, you may not see yourself as a professional facilitator, but you certainly need a high level of facilitation skill. In my work as a coach and consultant I hear many unvarnished accounts of truly terrible meetings. One client had been recently promoted and for all his extreme seniority confessed that he did not know how to run a proper meeting. One of the reasons was the poor standard of meetings' behaviour he observed in his organization. For instance, here he is describing the regular Monday morning meeting held by his boss

> The Managing Director assembles us. He has a vast office – in fact you could probably fit the whole of my flat into it. He sits at a 'top table' – a huge old-fashioned mahogany thing. He has his immediate Director team around him at the table. It's like a

school with him as the headmaster and The Directors as the teachers. In front of him, the rest of us sit in rows. We're the prefects. Then on the sides are some hangers on – too junior to have proper chairs so they often stand for the whole meeting. It's awful! Designed to make you feel ten years old again. No one speaks honestly. It's just a ritual and I hate it. No wonder that as an organisation we're so stuck.

When people see this kind of poor example, it makes it far more difficult for them to learn a more facilitative style themselves, but to do so is vital if you want more than lip service from the people you lead and manage.

5   Leaders of action-learning sets

Action learning was developed by Professor Reg Revans (1980) as an antidote to what he called 'programmed learning' – the kind of issue where there is a known solution. Programmed learning is the stuff of business schools with their neat case studies and happy endings. Action learning works where all the known solutions have been tried and failed. A 'set' – normally a group of senior people sponsored by their organizations, meets for a half day. Each person has the floor for an agreed period of time and presents a live problem – something that if not resolved will have major impact for them and for their organization. Expert listening on the part of other group members and expert facilitation by the set leader will create new levels of both support and challenge for the 'problem-holder'.

6   A life skill

In fact facilitation is a life skill, useful in all kinds of circumstances. Readers of the first edition of this book have sent me many accounts of being able to use facilitation skills informally.

> Two parents came in to school to complain about the lack of progress as they saw it of their child. The parents seemed aggressive. Previously I would have been frightened and dismayed or else just defensive and angry myself. However, I realised that facilitation was what was needed. Within a few minutes they had calmed right down and we were able to have a conversation which solved the problem amicably.
>
> (Headteacher, inner city school)

> The divorced parents of a close friend had to meet to agree on a very sad task. Their son had been killed and they wanted a

headstone for his grave. My friend was their surviving son. The divorce had been acrimonious and they were all still in shock and grief. My friend asked me to run the discussion – in effect to facilitate it. It was remarkably easy – by using facilitation skills we did it with no fuss and in a very short time.

I use it all the time. I have frequently deflected squabbles among friends or helped solve things like 'where shall we go today?' on holidays where everyone is dithering in a maddening way. One or two of them have noticed and refer to it as my 'sleight of hand' because they can't quite work out how it's done.

In the 11 years since the first edition of this book was published, the acknowledged need for facilitation skills has grown. However, I do not notice any differences in the worries, levels of skill and knowledge brought by participants on the courses where I teach facilitation skills. People still fret about the stubbornly silent participant, the mouthy know-it-all, the dangers of opening the dreaded *cans of worms* or what to do if it all goes horribly wrong.

The numbers of people who know they need these skills have increased as attitudes to management and leadership have shifted radically. Although there is obviously an important place for directive leadership, there is now a greater understanding that when faced with the severe challenges of organizational life a facilitative style will achieve more and in a shorter time.

How you do this is what the rest of this book is about. My aim has been to write about the reality rather than the theory of facilitation because practice leads theory in this field, as in so many others. I am a practitioner and this book reflects my 20 years of experience in this role and many before that as a teacher or trainer. It is based on what I have known to work. Like its predecessor edition, this one is deliberately short, designed to cut away as much of the confusing verbiage as possible around the subject while still doing justice to the complexity of the skills and knowledge you need.

1   What is facilitation?

Our remedies oft in ourselves do lie
Which we ascribe to Heaven.

(*All's Well that Ends Well*, William Shakespeare)

If I create from the heart, nearly everything works; if from the head, almost nothing.

(Mark Chagall, painter)

Facilitate means, literally, to make something easy. The purpose of facilitation is to make it easier for the group to learn. As a facilitator your aim is to work with the group towards their becoming more competent, more powerful and more in control of their own destinies.

Some examples are:

- A group that is facing up to the poor quality of its interpersonal relationships.
- A team that needs to agree a better strategy for dealing with customers.
- Two or more groups trying to understand how they can improve their working systems and relationships.
- A management team whose leader wants to see more joint sharing of responsibility.
- A negotiation of any kind where the two parties need to learn about the other side's point of view, as well as having the opportunity to put their own.

The need for facilitation

Facilitation is not the answer to every organizational problem. There is still a need for directive leadership. When the organization is in danger and there is a need for swift action, facilitated discussion may not be the answer. For instance, to take an extreme example, in a serious house fire, the fire crew does not stop to discuss how people feel: they issue clear, simple orders. In fast-moving environments it may sometimes be better to do unambiguous *telling*. When people are new, uncertain or untrained, it is often quicker, simpler, more effective and cheaper to direct them.

The changing climate in organizations

However, the climate in organizations is changing. There is no longer the assumption that bosses know best. Indeed, the most recent recession showed in shocking detail that in many of our formerly most respected organizations, their leaders not only did not know best but that their personal greed and lack of judgement was precisely what brought these organizations – and our economy – to such a state of difficulty. It is unlikely that people will ever again have the same kinds of automatic respect for their managers. At the same time, there are huge amounts of change to be managed. Even in times of economic growth, no organization stays the same for long – the pressures from competitors, government, customers and staff are all too strong. Most bosses now know that you cannot simply impose change and hope that people's protests will fade with time. More people than ever before have experienced higher education; virtually all employees now expect a high level of autonomy and insist on being consulted. Even in times of high unemployment, there are skill shortages. If you treat people badly, they will walk away, as this managing partner in a legal practice comments

> Lawyers are the original examples of how you can't herd cats. They may give you the outward appearance of being docile, but scratch the surface of compliance and they will yowl. Running this firm is like having many dozens of independent practitioners who happen to be graciously lending you their time and skill. You can't impose much. If you do they will just go to a competitor or start up on their own. A participative style is the only one that works and to do that I have had to learn how to be a facilitator. It helped when I went on a mediation course and I learnt what was involved in facilitation there and have been able to apply it productively to all my Practice meetings as well as in face to face work with clients.

Boundaries are blurring

Boundaries between departments no longer seem firm. For a department to be successful, it will inevitably have to work with other departments where possibly there are different kinds of people doing different kinds of work. Yet cooperation is often vital if both are to be successful. I worked with a department of technical specialists that was supplying services to another department in the same organization. Somehow, relationships had deteriorated. There were disputes about cross-charging and allegations on both sides of sloppiness. True, they had recruited different kinds of people and initially the staff were on different terms and conditions. Competition from the outside world began to bear on both. They could no longer expect the same steady flow of success that both had taken for granted in the past. Slowly the truth dawned: their fates actually hung together. In this case, there had to be a series of facilitated days together to work steadily at dismantling the misconceptions and hostilities of the past, and this could not be done by anyone seen to be associated with either team: a neutral facilitator was vital.

The same factors are even more obviously at work when the process involves working across organizations; for instance, providers of health services with local authority social service departments, working to ensure that the best use is made of limited public funds.

Greater transparency

It is far more difficult to bury mistakes and misdoings now than it was even a decade ago. Some organizations have 'whistleblower' policies, though I am dubious about how far these actually make it easy for whistles to be blown as it still seems to be the case that the whistleblowers are persecuted and excuses found to sack them. But if you see something obviously wrong in your organization, you may readily leak it to media eager for revelation and scandal. There are whole websites devoted to TheTruthAbout<anything you like>.com. As customers we are also more ready to complain and to persist, using any means at our disposal: blogs, newspapers, tweets . . . In the UK the Freedom of Information Act was explicitly passed in order to force organizations to disclose information deemed to be in the public interest. This has resulted in a great deal of squirming and indignant justifying as details of salaries, bonuses, dodgy deals and overgenerous expenses have been made public.

There are also more conventional routes to greater transparency. For instance, most large organizations now conduct regular staff surveys. Often the results are dismaying to senior managers, many of whom might have been fooling themselves about their own effectiveness and popularity, as this manager comments:

> My company did yet another staff survey. Overall the data was damning. People said they had no faith in the executive team, felt afraid to take decisions themselves for fear of draconian punishment

if they got it wrong and therefore funnelled every decision upwards. They took pride in their own work and liked their immediate colleagues but felt they were being managed by idiots. This time we could break down results by department so there was no hiding place.

Similarly, most organizations have publicly declared targets with all the overt pressure that this will create. Listed companies work under the glare of City analysts, shareholder meetings and of their own published financial results. Public sector organizations labour under the severe pressures of imposed targets; for instance, in the NHS to reduce waiting times. All this creates greater transparency and draws attention to the need for change.

Complexity

When organizations merge, close, downsize or change their market positions, these changes are perplexing to those in the middle of them. Even the people at the top of the organization can feel as if they are being pulled in many different directions at once. The likelihood is that no one can feel in control of the whole thing and that any sense of control is a delusion as this newly appointed chief executive commented:

> We were merging two companies, one British, one French. There were excellent commercial reasons for doing it but we knew it would be difficult: the language differences, national differences and legal systems, the radically different cultures in each of the organizations. But as soon as we started the actual process of creating a new culture for the merged company the reality became even more complicated and bewildering. Just simple things like whether people were prepared to travel on a Sunday night, for instance, for a Monday morning meeting: the British were, the French were not!

The elephant in the room

Team members often collude with one another to maintain a difficulty of some kind but an outsider will see it immediately. This is the 'elephant in the room' (see Figure 1.1), an issue so big and overwhelming that no one ever refers to it openly, yet it is assumed by the group to be an immovable block to progress. Examples could be:

- a fiercely fought rivalry between two senior people
- a generally low standard of work

Figure 1.1
Source: Chris Radley.

- the strong possibility that a unit will be disbanded
- a leader who is not respected
- a team member who is widely regarded as unable to do her work

Here is an example from my own practice:

> The boss believed that he had an unruly team who simply wouldn't see the world his way. An awayday was arranged and I was hired as facilitator. Like the rest of the group, I discovered at 9 20 am for a 9 30 am start that the boss in question had accepted a lobbyist's invitation to all-day hospitality at an international football match, leaving me with the group. The group was outraged at his rudeness, as indeed was I, and it was soon clear that they were outraged at many other things as well. The dialogue went like this:

Group member 1:	'Shall we talk about It or not?'
	[Silence]
Group member 2:	'You mean him? [Long silence] I don't know. Can we trust our facilitator?'
Me:	Anything you say to me here is confidential, though we will of course need to discuss how you take any serious issues forward with X (name of boss).
Group member 3:	'Well what have we got to lose? Let's go for it!'

The elephant was well and truly named here, and once spoken in front of an outsider, it could not be ignored again. That day started a process that ended with that particular manager leaving the organization when it was clear he simply could not change a style, which had put him at odds with not only his immediate team but also with his own bosses.

When is facilitation the answer?

All the factors above create the circumstances where facilitation might be needed. If you are wondering whether this is true for any project in which you might be involved, these are the typical conditions where it is so valuable:

- No one knows the answer.
- No one has all the power.
- There is an enormous amount of confusion and complexity around whatever the presenting problem seems to be.
- The problems are systemic and are unlikely to be solved through a familiar quick fix.

- You want commitment, not just compliance.
- There is a high level of negative emotion: anger, anxiety, fear.
- You are working at the leading edge of some great change and there is no neat theory to explain it.
- Long-term relationships matter and will be compromised by quick fixes or bogus agreements.
- Collaboration is the only way forward.

Professional facilitators may be people from inside or outside the organization, but it is better to be outside rather than inside the group. This is because one of your main values as a facilitator is your separateness. You have no emotional commitment to the group in its everyday tasks and roles. You will be able to see things that they cannot and will have permission to raise matters that they will find difficult.

Facilitation creates a climate where it is possible to ask for everyone's ideas. Groups regularly produce higher-quality responses than any one individual can. Equally importantly, facilitation produces buy-in. This principle has been known for many years. A study during World War II compared the responses of two groups of women to advice about feeding their families. Those who were lectured about the correct diet were significantly less likely to take up the advice than those who were part of facilitated groups where there was discussion. Senior people are often initially worried about the violent objections that they anticipate their people will make to some proposal for change. But discussing the objections is always the first step to finding approaches to managing the change in a way that people will accept rather than fight.

What facilitation is not

Facilitation is not the same as some other activities that may look superficially similar, though several of these activities benefit from a facilitative approach (see Table 1.1).

Facilitators and trainers

Being a facilitator is different from being a trainer, though as a trainer you facilitate discussions and as a facilitator your aim is learning. However, as a facilitator, your aim is not to transfer knowledge from yourself to participants. Nor is it to follow a set timetable or to feel that you always have to be in control. There is no element of assessment against agreed standards and no curriculum that must be followed. The assumption is that people already have the resources they need to move on – your role is to mobilize those resources as quickly as possible.

Chairing a meeting	Usually has an end point connected with a specific task such as briefing people, agreeing a decision
Guided discussion as part of a course	May be genuine facilitation, but more often is legitimately leading people to a set of 'right' and 'wrong' answers around a specific piece of information
Chairing a debate	Confrontational format is designed to overemphasize differences in order to explore an issue
Group therapy	Group therapists work with people who are, or feel they are, dysfunctional. No such assumption is made about facilitation, though therapists working with groups may have to use facilitation skills and some members of such groups may be, or feel, dysfunctional

Table 1.1

As a trainer, you are assumed to have knowledge about the subject. As a facilitator, you may have none. A colleague was once asked if he would facilitate a high-level discussion for a group in an industry of which he knew literally nothing. He says the discussion swirled around him all day with people talking about their technical concerns without him having any idea what the content was. He had been understandably anxious about the day in advance, yet this was still a highly successful day – 'It was pure facilitation', he said proudly.

Facilitators and leaders

A leader will often need to operate in facilitative mode, but this is different from being a facilitator *per se*. A leader is responsible for the group's task and its outputs and has line management responsibility for their performance. A facilitator is outside such responsibilities and may therefore be able to say things in public to the leader that would not be possible for anyone else. A facilitator being present allows the leader to join in the event just like anyone else. And bear in mind that the leader is invariably part of the problem as well as part of the solution. However, knowing how to use facilitation techniques is a vital part of any leader's toolkit: the quality of your meetings will improve and you will be able to manage change more swiftly and effectively.

Internal versus external facilitators

This need to be – and be seen to be – neutral can complicate the task of facilitation.

When you are an internal facilitator you have a number of advantages. You know the culture and the people; no one will need to explain the mysterious acronyms of the organization to you. You will have a password to the intranet and you will have effortless access to senior people. Follow-up will be dozens of times easier than it is for an external facilitator: you will have innumerable unforced ways of seeking further feedback and making suggestions for future events, a huge advantage, as one of the main concerns when you are an external facilitator is the frustration of running only one event, on grounds of cost, when both you and the client can see that there is actually a need for a continuing programme. Not least, although there might be some cross-charging involved, the likelihood is that your services will be free, making it an attractive proposition for clients to hire you. At the same time, all these advantages are also weaknesses. The very familiarity of the culture makes it likely that you will share the same blindspots as your clients. Here is one facilitator describing the different perspective she immediately saw on this after she had left her organization:

> It wasn't until I left that I realised how handicapped I'd been by knowing it all so well. As soon as I started working for other organisations as a facilitator I understood that things I'd taken for granted as 'can'ts' and 'don'ts' were peculiar to us. For instance, it was taken for granted that you could never contradict a senior editor because they were the Gods. I was very timid with these people. I soon saw that as an outsider where you didn't share this fear perhaps because you didn't truly understand the hierarchy, you could and should be much bolder and that these were often the very people whom it was essential to challenge.

As an internal facilitator you also have to accept the consequences of the day. If it goes well, that's great, but if it appears to go badly, you have to live with the consequences; you cannot just shrug and walk away knowing that other clients will be along soon. You may also be over-affected by hierarchical considerations, believing that if you are paid less and on a lower grade than your clients, you cannot take risks; for instance, through confrontation and challenge.

External facilitators may have the glamour of their known work with other organizations. The useful knowledge that comes with this background is often highly valued by clients. As an external you take nothing for granted and are remarkably free of hierarchical assumptions and in my own case, where clients have offered to explain the intricacies of their grading system to me, I have begged them not to. I approach each event assuming that everyone present potentially has something valid to offer, regardless of hierarchical position. In fact, I am aware from experience that this can be insignificant when real influence is what matters. For instance, most chief executives have a person in their team with some kind of meaningless title and no managerial responsibilities to speak of. Yet this character is often the one with a great deal of informal power. All post-war British prime ministers have had such a person in their entourage, mostly without cabinet responsibilities, and have bowed to their judgements. At the same time, you have none of the comfortable advantages of the internal provider. It is more difficult to gain entry to the organization; indeed, you may have to go through an agonizingly tortuous tendering process to get the work in the first place. Your fees are a cash cost to the organization and this is often a discouragement to commissioning more work, even when it is clearly necessary.

I have worked as both an internal and external facilitator and despite the above see little difference in practice because everything depends on skill and on the well-grounded confidence that goes with it. You can have this irrespective of whether you are an employee or a freelance. Some of the most successful facilitators I know work internally, their skills prized by their employers and constantly in demand. And we can probably all recall innumerable anecdotal examples, described to us by their appalled clients, of externals whose skills were woefully lacking despite the high fees they charged.

The importance of the human process

Facilitation is special because it is about both task and human process. Task is about whatever the group has agreed it must achieve – its outputs. Most groups feel comfortable with their task. They know they have to agree a decision, plan a project or write a report. The concept of human process is much more often ignored. Process concerns feelings that may or may not be expressed and visible. Neglect of the process aspects of group life can swiftly derail a group. (I explore the origins and concept of process more fully in Chapter 2.)

One way of looking at this was developed by Bill Evans and his author colleagues Peter Cockman and Peter Reynolds, explained in their book *Consulting for Real People* (Cockman et al., 1999). Bill himself refers to it informally as the 'hamburger model' though it does not have this racy title in his book.

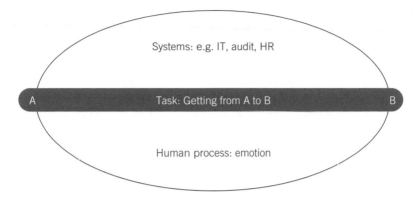

Figure 1.2   The 'hamburger model' of organizations
Source: This figure was adapted with kind permission from Cockman et al. (1999).

The model represents organizational life where the upper part of the 'bun' stands for systems and processes. These will include finance, information technology (IT), human resources (HR), quality and audit. Typical questions associated with systems might include:

- How do we monitor what we are spending?
- What's the best way to recruit or let people go?
- How do we track our customers, who they are and what they spend?
- What software do we need to commission to make our business efficient?

The 'meat' in the middle is task: how we get from A to B and all the milestones, roles and accountabilities that will help get us there. Typical questions here could be:

- Who should play which part in this project?
- How quickly do we need to see results? What are the deadlines?
- How much money will it cost to deliver what's needed?
- What other resources do we need?

Everyone in organizations understand and can see the need for both systems and tasks: they are familiar, measurable and therefore reassuring. They represent rationality, logic, order and control. The world's major management consultancies specialize in providing services to deal with these issues; for instance, offering business process redesign, data collection and analysis, help with restructuring or with the design and delivery of IT projects.

So how is it then that so many change projects in organizations fail miserably? How is it, for instance, that one notorious government-commissioned IT project is currently billions overspent and years behind schedule? What can explain the reality that a high percentage (60 per cent, 70 per cent, 80 per cent – no one really has a clue about the true percentage, so take your pick, but make the number high) of change projects, particularly those charged with transforming the culture of the organization, never achieve what they set out to do? The reason is clear: it is all that messy stuff labelled 'human process' – the lower 'bun' of the 'hamburger'.

The human process is about feelings, not rationality. You will certainly hear some people allege that they 'leave feelings at home' when they come to work. But work stirs up emotion and why wouldn't it when so much of our identity and satisfaction is bound up in it? Elements that come into play with the human process will include:

- how people feel about their bosses
- whether or not people feel secure about their own and the organization's future
- levels of openness, trust and accessibility to senior managers
- how performance is managed, how clearly standards are set and what the consequences are for achievement and failure; who gets promoted and why
- how decisions are really made rather than the fictions that are commonly described
- how differences of gender, sexual orientation, social class, age, physical disability, race and religion are actually handled; that is, when the organizational police who wrote the Equalities Policy are not looking
- how much involvement and consultation there is
- levels of investment in training and development and who gets the opportunities to take part
- how the official values in the organization fit with the values its people see actually practised

Any one of these issues has the potential for strong emotion and in every organization all of them are at play. People are imperfect and the people who run organizations more often get it wrong than right because it is actually so hard to get all of it right all of the time, so some disappointment, disillusion and anger are the norm.

The trouble is that where task and systems can be analysed, written down and measured, it is much harder to see and measure the human process. It is messy and ambiguous. Staff may feel one thing but say another; for instance, they may complain angrily to a friend in the corridor outside a meeting but play compliant serf inside it. Bosses do not want to hear bad news and they especially do not want to hear about their own unpopularity and incompetence. All this conspires to make the human process ever present but invisible and therefore easy to ignore – until there is a crisis when finally it has to be faced.

I was contacted by a client at the BBC about a culture-change project. I asked what he had already done to solve the problems of his department.

> 'Those', he said laconically, jerking his head towards a long shelf jammed with thick folders behind him.
> 'What are they?'
> 'Four years-worth of reports from [insert name of any large consultancy] which resulted in precisely nothing happening.'
> 'And the reason?'
> 'People! People dragging their feet, people complaining and whining, people leaving; people being moved on before they could take sensible action; the unions protesting, people being afraid they'd lose their jobs, not wanting to change comfortable ways . . . Shall I go on?!'

I have to say in defence of these distinguished consultancies that my project

Figure 1.3
Source: © Steven Appleby (2006a).

was not really that much more productive – my client, like so many of his predecessors, was reorganized and moved to a different role and shortly afterwards left the BBC.

Failure to deal successfully with the human process results in the failure of most change projects. When there is something going on that we do not like, we are experts in sabotage: asking for more data, failing to follow up on decisions, complaining about overwork, going off sick with that all-encompassing, vague 'illness': stress; writing action plans rather than doing the actions; ignoring requests; having tantrums; making threats; lodging grievances . . . the list is literally endless. In fact, when faced with difficulties over the human process, most bosses are inclined to try to solve it with a system, as this manager described:

> No one in our organisation is willing to face up to poor performance. There is a belief, frankly wrong, that you can't sack anyone so there's no point in giving feedback. Add to that the general embarrassment at tackling another person about the standard of their work and people will do anything rather than confront. Mediocre performance is the norm. So, guess what? The Chief Executive decides to commission a new appraisal system. It was introduced. People saw it as a tick box exercise so it quickly fell into disuse like all its predecessors. This is because it's an organisational culture problem of feelings and attitudes and you can't solve those with a system, however good it seems to be.

The writer and consultant Chris Argyris (1990) has offered us the notion of 'skilled incompetence'. In his familiar descriptions of how organizational defences get in the way of learning and improvement, he suggests that our need to feel in control is at odds with the reality of human shortcomings. When embarrassed or threatened, we do not behave according to the values we espouse, but revert to the more primitive states of wanting to win at all costs, of saving face and suppressing negative feelings. We bypass errors but then make the bypass undiscussable because errors cannot be bypassed once they are discussable. So the undiscussability of the undiscussable is also undiscussable. This requires enormous skill in trying to do essentially unproductive things; for instance, changing someone's mind without upsetting them, or realizing that although organizational performance is suffering, it would be too embarrassing to face up to the negative emotions that discussing it would create. In this way, truth is distorted and defences grow. As a result, people will moan vigorously about the organization without accepting any personal responsibility for failure. These alleged shortcomings in the organization can then get exaggerated in order to justify our own learned helplessness in dealing with them.

In his book *The Five Dysfunctions of Team* (2002) Patrick Lencioni offers a powerful model showing how a pyramid of emotional dysfunction leads relentlessly to poor performance. At the base of the pyramid is absence of trust, characterized by people who pose as being tough and vulnerable. The next level is fear of conflict, where the fear is masked by the appearance of harmony, leading as you go up the pyramid to lack of commitment to team results then avoidance of accountability and tolerance of low standards. Finally, at the apex, is the ultimate result: inattention to results characterized by a preoccupation with individual status and ego. This is a potent model to bring to leaders, some of whom are inclined to assert that what they dismissively refer to as 'touchy-feely stuff' is a nice-to-have option, irrelevant to business results. As one client said to me worriedly, his team facing annihilation because of their poor performance, 'I do hope we're not all going to be lying on the floor holding hands on this awayday'. This told me that some kind of hand-holding, either physical or metaphorical, was probably exactly what was needed, though of course I soothed his fears at the time.

Many groups need help at the base of the pyramid because they will be presenting a public face of invulnerability. What is really going on here is absence of trust and trust is the foundation on which all teamwork has to be built. Absence of trust is characterized by a dread of meetings, guardedness, hiding mistakes and uncertainties, inability to ask each other for help and criticizing the character and motivation of other team members. As you ascend the pyramid, you pass successively through the pretence of harmony, ambiguity about direction and priorities, avoiding holding each other to account, leading ultimately to inattention to results. The instinct of many leaders when faced with the stark reality of poor results is to try doing more of what has already failed – typically draconian command-and-control, whereas what may actually be needed is to start at the fundamentals: how can we build trust?

This is prime territory for facilitators. The human process is the essence of what you deal with. You specialize in working with people to surface, name, face and manage the feelings that are getting in the way of accomplishing the tasks or making the systems work. You go where others have been too timid or too blind. The aim is to change attitudes, beliefs and ultimately behaviour. That is what makes it such a demanding and fascinating role.

Facilitation involves:

- leading because you are trusted, not because you have formal authority; leading with the confidence that comes from being at peace with yourself
- behaving in a way that encourages disclosure

- being willing to listen to all members of the group without being affected by status, gender or other preconceptions about who and what people are
- wanting to understand; suspending judgement
- being willing to be divergent rather than convergent when appropriate
- being able to keep any number of different points of view in front of the group for as long as seems necessary; keeping track of issues that someone has raised but which have not been pursued
- creating the right blend of challenge and support for group members
- creating a climate that ensures members share their diverse knowledge and experience
- creating a climate of warmth where it is all right to own up to weakness and to ask for help
- helping group members to develop insights into themselves and others
- helping group members to develop emotional resilience
- confronting blockages and working with the group to find creative ways around them
- drawing attention to and helping to manage the emotional aspects of whatever the group is doing; making it all right to express feelings as well as facts
- working flexibly across a range of styles, approaches and techniques

This is a daunting list. As I have become a more experienced facilitator myself, I have come to realize the truth of the saying that less is more where facilitation is concerned. It often seems to me that some of the most effective facilitators I know are the ones who apparently do least. David Casey puts it well in his book *Managing Learning in Organizations* ([1993] 1996):

> The great secret is to remember why you are there and why you are about to make your intervention. An intervention has one purpose only – to facilitate learning. Not to demonstrate your own amazing powers of perception, not to put someone in her place, not to rescue a lame duck, not to impress, not to generate dependency, but only to help learning take place. This is the sole motivation which has validity as I see it. Holding on to that single-minded aim helps me enormously. In particular, it helps during all those times when you do not intervene, when you bite your lip, sit on your hands and wait to see if learning will take place without your intervention – knowing that if it will, any intervention on your part would be wasteful of a precious asset, could generate dependency and might take from some

other member of the group the chance to intervene in their own way. So my own rule in simple: intervene as little as possible and only when you believe learning will result.

Some underpinning assumptions and principles

Clients will sometimes invite you to facilitate an event, making it clear that they have already decided both the agenda and the outcomes. I was once approached by a manager who explained that my role would be to 'facilitate' the staff conference – a yearly two-day ritual to which 150 people were invited. Further discussion revealed that what she really wanted me to do was to chair a set piece performance, perhaps much like most international summit conferences where the real work has been done behind the scenes in advance, the bland words of the communiqué already drafted. A complete agenda had already been devised, most of it consisting of worthy lectures with five minutes left at the end of each session for respectful questions to the speaker. My client explained that even in the panel discussion, which was to end the event, the questioners and their questions had already been chosen and the answers rehearsed. I courteously suggested that she would be better off with one of the many high-profile media presenters who make a good living doing just this kind of job with great skill and charm.

It is a mistake, by the way, to believe that participants do not see straight through such intentions. An elaborate and expensive set of conferences was set up in one organization where the chief executive was grossly unpopular with staff. The aim of the conferences was to sell the organization his strategy, a project heralded by glossily printed brochures, a copy of which had gone to every member of staff only to be received with hoots of derision and tart questions about what it had cost. It was mandatory to attend the conferences. It was believed, rightly, that both the nature of the organization's problems and their solutions had already been decided and that 'participation' and 'consultation' were fictions. This initiative was then duly sabotaged by the cynicism of those attending, whose mocking praise was confined to the excellence of the lunch.

Eight principles of authentic facilitation

True facilitation is different. I believe that there are eight principles that underlie the kind of facilitation that will underpin any of the skills and tactics that you need to employ.

1 *Facilitation is about change*

A facilitated event is always about change. Most probably this will have been triggered by external factors such as new regulations, competitor activity, and economic and social forces. Any such change has the potential to induce feelings of helplessness and bewilderment. All the obvious tactics will already have been tried and will have failed. If nothing needs to change then you do not need a facilitator. Most frequently, the client group knows it needs to change but does not know how to make it happen. Or perhaps it *need*s to change but draws back because contemplating the change is complex and frightening. Part of your role will therefore be to encourage the group to name and face up to its biggest challenges, not to duck them. The purpose of any facilitated event is to increase the commitment of participants to the changes they want and need to make and to increase their feelings of autonomy.

> *Implications for facilitators:* you must be able to offer feedback, interruption and challenge. This also means that the action-planning phase that normally ends a facilitated event is not just a pointless charade but the beginnings of different behaviour. If change remains only at the level of intellectual understanding and does not involve behaviour then nothing will be different.

2 *You need facilitation when the issue is a 'wicked' and not a 'simple' problem*

The distinction between wicked and simple problems was first made by a teacher of social planning and architecture, Horst Rittel, in the early 1970s but it applies to any complex issue. A simple problem is one where there is an easy, obvious solution; one right answer. A wicked problem is one that may even be difficult to define for certain – there may be a lack of agreement about what the problem actually is. It is also one where every apparently obvious solution for one group or person would also have a negative impact on someone else, and the problem itself will usually turn out to be just a symptom of some other underlying set of problems. Wicked problems are never truly solved because they are knotted and complex, their multiple causes usually deep-rooted in the quick-fix solutions of the past. And each one is unique, so ready-made answers are unlikely to work. At the global level, most social and environmental problems are examples of wicked problems; for instance, climate change, the AIDS epidemic and drug trafficking. With climate change, for instance, it may seem obvious to us in the first world that we have to reduce carbon emissions, but this will most probably be resisted by the fast-growing economies of India or China where a cheap old-style carbon-unfriendly car has so many obvious advantages. The real give-away to determine whether your group is facing a wicked or a simple problem is to ask about their stakeholders – the individuals or groups whose opinion can affect the outcome of any decision. Characteristically, where the problems are wicked, the stakeholders will have dramatically different needs and opposing opinions that can most probably never be reconciled.

> *Implications for facilitators:* the focus for the group will be on searching for the solution, even if it is never found. Your focus has to be on helping the group deepen its commitment to making some sort of progress through working together. Often this will mean finding a solution that is *good enough* rather than perfect. This is why it is so important that you have working knowledge of human learning and group dynamics. It is also why it is important to take a broad, systemic perspective and to help ensure that the group looks at the problem in its context, especially externally.

3 *Clients are resourceful: underneath their hesitations and fears they do know what to do*

This point was first made helpfully explicit in relation to organizational groups in 1969 by the US writer and consultant Edgar Schein in his book *Process Consultation Revisited*, a new edition of which appeared in 1999, but it descends in a straight line from the mid-twentieth-century pioneer of humanistic psychology and counselling, Carl Rogers. It involves accepting that the client group will know more about their situation than you ever will and that they, not you, will have to live with whatever decisions they make. The facilitation process is about working with the client to identify the client's understanding of what is right and wrong and gives the client permission to act on that understanding.

> *Implications for facilitators:* you do not need to be an expert on your client's core business. They are the experts. You do not need to feel responsible for finding solutions: that is their role. If they do not find solutions, you have to be able to live with the ambiguity and discomfort: it is their choice, not yours. This is why you must hone your process skills because they are what you bring to the event.

4 *It is a relationship of equals*

If your role is to engage clients' resourcefulness not to offer them solutions, then unlike traditional consulting where the models are what Schein calls 'expert helper' or 'doctor–patient', the relationship of equality with the client or client group is at the core. Clients bring their willingness to engage in the problem and their knowledge of the context; you bring your facilitation skills. Facilitators also have equal respect for every participant regardless of any of the markers of differing status that normally distinguish human beings one from the other.

Implications for facilitators: hierarchy, though an important factor in understanding the organization, is irrelevant in terms of your relationship with the group. Many senior leaders are determinedly unaware of how they strike people. If they create dread in those they manage, you cannot afford to react in the same way. Your value is in being able to approach them as one human being to another without fear or a need to flatter, deceive or cajole. The most senior person present is just another participant: beware of any tendency to give them more airtime or to indulge their delusions. Similarly, you cannot afford to share any condescension levelled at the juniors in a team. Often the most junior people are the ones who have the best ideas about how to solve organizational problems because they are far more likely to have direct contact with its customers. Your role is to enable everyone to be heard regardless of age or seniority.

5 *These are authentic, whole-person conversations where feelings can be expressed*

True facilitation is about being able to engage the group in conversations that are authentic. This means that such conversations may be edgy, difficult and challenging as well as containing humour and laughter. You are being real, bringing your whole selves to the conversation, not just some well-defended public relations (PR) front – and remember this applies as much to you as to the group. The purpose is to talk about everything that matters, including the topics that have been skilfully avoided thus far, including people's fears and need for help. The cartoonist, Jacky Fleming, has a drawing where the man sits frowning, his arms folded, saying, 'You're so emotional'. The woman, not looking at him, is replying dryly, 'An obvious shortcoming for a human being I suppose'.

Implications for facilitators: A group often moves on when its individual members can admit to vulnerability. Encourage the recognition that 'feelings are facts' – how you feel about something is every bit as important as what the facts are about it. Having the courage to design well-judged activities where feelings can be expressed is all part of the role. Knowing how to manage the moment where feelings surface is an essential skill that starts with the assumption on your own part that emotion is legitimate and necessary.

6 *The facilitator is neutral*

Facilitators do not and cannot take sides because they will not be involved in implementing the decisions that are taken. When fiercely held opposing views are expressed in a group, the group can quickly get stuck in its familiar polarized positions. When you have a stake in the outcome, you may do your best to conceal your opinion but nonetheless you will be assumed by all present to have one. Being seen to be neutral is therefore a huge advantage. Note, however, that neutral does not mean unassertive.

Implications for facilitators: your job is to explore what lies behind the stances that people are taking. What are the areas of agreement; what kind of territory lies in between? This is not usually possible when you are far inside the issues and the group.

7 *Facilitation involves simultaneous high support and high challenge for participants*

True facilitation involves the toughness and steadiness that comes from willingness to work at all times in the top-right quadrant of Figure 1.4. If your work involves only high challenge it will come across as abrasive impatience, or if it is a softer version of the same behaviour, it will involve advice-giving. This invariably leads to defensiveness: *you don't understand.* If you do low challenge and low support, the discussion descends into a meaningless chat

High challenge

Abrasive; advice-giving
Impact: defensiveness

True facilitation
Impact: increased
openness to change

Low support ——————————————————————— **High support**

Meaningless chat
Impact: indifference

Soggy emotionalism
Impact: helplessness

Low challenge

Figure 1.4   The support and challenge matrix

and the impact on participants is indifference. In the bottom-right quadrant, you are at risk of implying that people are helpless victims, making it unlikely that they will be able to embrace change. Most of us will inhabit all three of these undesirable quadrants at some point when building our experience as facilitators.

> *Implications for facilitators:* you must be willing to work with empathy, to suspend judgement (high support) and also be able to offer challenge through techniques such as offering feedback, creating space for unheard voices, or asking participants to examine their cherished assumptions.

8 *Work in the moment*

Turning points in a facilitated event most frequently come from being able to work 'in the moment'. This means noticing, commenting on and working with the data that the group generates in the room; for instance, its patterns of interaction. This contrasts vividly with the way most organizational discussion happens where the focus is either on brooding about the past (often what we or you did wrong) or on speculation about the future (how things might turn out, for instance, how wonderful our strategic plan is; how it will deliver us from our enemies) or on some trivial operational detail and all this virtually always at the level of apparent rationality.

> *Implications for facilitators:* this is why the skill of being able to work with the human process, noticing it, offering respectful feedback and encouraging the group to do the same is so powerful.

It is tough to adhere to these principles because to do so needs exceptional levels of maturity and steadiness. When done well, the skills of facilitation look invisible. When done badly, its failings are painfully apparent.

2　The secret life of groups

When all think alike, no-one thinks very much.

(Walter Lippman, US commentator)

Few people are capable of expressing with equanimity opinions which differ from the prejudices of their social environment.

(Albert Einstein, physicist)

All groups have a secret life. Our collective behaviour is strikingly different from the way we as the individuals in the group will behave when on our own. You need to know about this secret life as a way of making sense of some of the otherwise baffling behaviour you will encounter.

We are a herd species. Our survival from the earliest days of Homo sapiens has depended on living in groups and it still does. To be banished from the herd is the most terrible punishment we can suffer short of death, because one of our most fundamental needs is to belong. Bullying always involves exclusion, whether among children or adults and its unbearable message is 'you are an outsider'. We also need leaders. The so-called *self-managing group* is an impossibility in practice. If there is no leader we will mewl and manoeuvre until we have forced someone to accept the role. We also seem hardwired to have in-groups and out-groups because in the tough struggle for food and territory as we emerged in prehistoric times 150,000 years ago, it must have been necessary to defend our own tribe against threats from other tribes. The evolutionary psychologists claim that since we have not faced any significant environmental challenge since that time, our brains and typical psychological responses are essentially the same. This is why attempts to eliminate racism and prejudice of any kind are utterly doomed, whatever the noble intentions of equality initiatives. We are natural experts at 'spot the difference'.

At the same time, our most spectacular successes, even when led by individuals of genius, have depended on our ability to cooperate in groups, our outstanding achievements created when highly dissimilar individuals can learn to manage their differences, seeing such differences as strengths, not threats. I observe that in practice this is very difficult to do and believe that the natural state of most human groups, whether families or work teams, is a dysfunction of one kind or another. This is because our need to belong, and therefore to suppress dissent, constantly rubs against our equally strong need to have things on our own terms and our need for this autonomy is constantly tested by our other equally strong need for the safety and dependency offered by submitting to a leader.

A group that seems to have a high level of what is usually called 'team spirit' may be particularly prone to making bizarrely poor decisions because its members suppress their private opinions out of fear that they may be ejected from the group. The quality of group thinking may be routinely deplorable. When we are members of a group we may endorse decisions we would not make individually. We may take risks that we would consider unacceptable if we were assessing such risks alone. We may agree to ignore a path of action that would seem obviously beneficial if assessing it for ourselves. As a facilitator you will be nose to nose with all of this. It is your job not just to understand it but also to point it out to the group and to work with them to manage it, challenging and supporting, with all the attendant risks; for instance, the group turning on you as the interloper – how dare you question them – or of you becoming sucked into the group's own world of obfuscation and delusion.

There are three aspects of group life that is worth exploring: how whole groups behave, how individuals in the group behave, and your own choice of style as facilitator.

Whole group behaviour

Lewin, Bion and the psychodynamic approach

Clarity about group behaviour has emerged from a richly tangled skein of thinkers and practitioners. Charles Darwin, Sigmund Freud, Carl Jung, Melanie Klein, Carl Rogers and many others have all helped us see how unconscious processes are at work when we are members of a group. This way of thinking began to appear in a more finessed form in the middle of the twentieth century. The political and social forces that created the two major wars – and their aftermaths – were the crucible that made such ideas possible. The phrase *group dynamics* was first used by one of the most illustrious people in this field, Kurt Lewin, a German-Jewish refugee from Nazi Germany who came to Britain in the tense period before World War II. Lewin's (1948) thinking has permeated an astonishing number of aspects of organizational theory and practice. To name just a few, his concept *force field analysis* (p. 95) is still regarded as fundamental to diagnosing how to handle organizational change; his action experiments on leadership have influenced every significant theorist who followed him. Lewin's work is relevant to facilitators because it proved beyond doubt that the same group will behave differently if led in different ways. In other words, the style of leadership is one of the most critical variables in predicting group behaviour. This is important information in two ways. As a facilitator you are also a leader. And there will also be a leader, or leaders, in the groups with whom you are working.

Wilfred Bion (1961) was a British psychiatrist and psychoanalyst who was one of the founders of the still-flourishing Tavistock Institute in London. After a bewildering and unhappy childhood, he fought as a 17-year-old in World War I, joining a tank regiment at a time when tanks were death traps from which few emerged alive. He survived a tank attack and was awarded the Distinguished Service Order (DSO). His ideas about groups were deeply influenced by the intense fear and sense of unreality that war created in him. Later in his life he believed that the group therapist/facilitator had to be able to *think under fire*, remaining cool, something he had been literally obliged to do in battle. As a doctor and psychiatrist in World War II, Bion was responsible for two influential and original ideas. First, he suggested that the War Office should use group processes to select officers, a notion that has led directly to the widespread use of assessment centres for all types of job today. Second, he developed psychotherapeutic groups for military personnel who had what we would now call post traumatic stress disorder, thus laying the foundation for what became *group therapy, encounter groups, self-development groups, large group awareness training, 'brainwashing'* in cults and dozens of other forms of group learning and activity. Bion also valued trusting his own emotional reactions to group behaviour, seeing them as vital data; advice that is still essential to any facilitator today.

Bion believed that groups inevitably descend into a kind of psychosis. His own writings can be dense and elliptical, but his thinking on the subject is well conveyed by Professor Robert M. Young, a thoughtful disciple, on his website[1]:

> I have worked a lot in groups. Indeed, for a period I did so as a matter of political faith. My experience was that, sure enough, from time to time each group would fall into a species of madness and start arguing and forming factions over matters which, on later reflection, would not seem to justify so much passion and distress. More often than not, the row would end up in a split or in the departure or expulsion of one or more scapegoats. This happened all over the place . . . Every time this happened to groups of which I was a member I thought it was either my fault or that I had once again fallen among thieves, scoundrels, zealots, dim-wits or some combination of the above. When I

read Bion I finally had a theoretical perspective on these processes. Moreover, he said that such debacles were inescapable, and they inevitably rope in the leader or facilitator. The trick is to be able to think under fire, to keep some part of your mind able to reflect on experience while having experience. If the group – or at least some of its members – can learn from experience and apply that learning to new situations, they can, just about, keep some semblance of the peace.

Bion's ideas were influenced by Freud and earlier psychoanalytical theories about the family. In turn, his own ideas have influenced virtually all subsequent thinkers about group dynamics. He, like Lewin, was among the first to propose that the group's task and its unconscious preoccupations are two separate elements happening in parallel. He suggested that groups quickly create their own culture, norms and roles as a defence against the anxieties of the unknown. Groups accept their undertaking at the conscious level – he called this the *work group*, the overt task. The work group is logical, sensible and acts according to openly agreed rules and procedures. Running alongside in every group is what he called a *basic assumption group*. He labelled it *basic* because its emotions are intense, primitive, roiling anxieties and *assumption* because the group behaves as if it believes its unconscious fantasies and flawed assumptions to be true. When a group is in basic assumption mode, the time boundaries disappear; skilled dialogue is avoided along with refusing to accept personal responsibility for what is happening in the group. Dysfunction follows. Bion identified three types of basic assumption group: dependence, flight/fight and pairing.

Dependence
The group has a leader and wants to be dependent on the leader, expecting the leader to look after them. It yearns for the magic of simplistic solutions and for the leader to take all the responsibility, yet it also wants to shake loose from the leader because the leader clips the freedom of individuals and constantly disappoints as of course any imperfect human being eventually will. He or she cannot be the messiah that the group wants. So the group attempts sabotage by providing misleading information, or acts out in subtle or overtly hostile ways. If the leader is unable to focus the group on its task, group members will seek to oust the leader and then become preoccupied with finding a replacement where the same process starts all over again. We may note that the careers of virtually all political leaders follow this trajectory. The shameless nature of political ambition nakedly exposes the dynamics. By the time the shortcomings of the 'dying' leader are obvious, the manoeuvring to find the new leader has already begun.

Fight/flight

The group believes it faces enemies. These enemies could be internal or external but it is better to believe you have enemies than to look critically at yourselves. The only options are to fight or to run away. Weaknesses are ruthlessly highlighted and a scapegoat is found to bear the burden of failure, real or apparent. The scapegoat may be inside or outside the group and if inside, like the failed leader, may be sidelined or hounded out.

When the group is in *flight* mode, it will retreat from the overt task, perhaps distracting itself with laughing and joking or going off on tangents. As a facilitator you may see the group wanting to take extended breaks, or even retreating from the work altogether, as in this vivid example, described to me by a colleague:

> I was tutor-facilitator on a leadership development course for an organisation that had decided it had a 'leadership crisis'. It was true that it did. The organisation had few leadership role models that its staff respected and if you became a manager you were widely considered to have 'sold out' or 'become one of The Suits'. All the participants were very senior people but it was soon clear that none was truly a volunteer. It was summer, a hot day and we were in a pleasant residential venue near Stratford on Avon. A delegation from the group came to see me at lunchtime to announce that they had decided to go en masse to a matinee at the Royal Shakespeare Theatre rather than be at the course. Barely disguising their glee they told me that this was justified on the grounds that the play was Henry V 'so it's all about leadership'!

Pairing

A pair, or several pairs in the group, becomes the focus of the group's hopes. Much faith is expressed in the creative effort that the pair can provide but usually this, too, will disappoint. The general sense is that somehow things will magically improve once this solution has come to pass: 'Things will be fine when we move to the new building', or 'Once we've appointed a customer services manager, the level of complaints will drop'. The pairing solution means that the group can avoid tackling its discontents and failures in the here and now.

In all basic assumption groups, which is all groups to some extent, Bion suggested that there will be strong emotion: love, hate, intense feelings of companionship or abhorrence. He pointed out how frequently there may be long silences or a feeling that there is something hidden that is waiting to be discovered. Fantasies about the motives and character of other group members may be projected from one to the other. Alliances are constantly shifting, forming and reforming as people seek approval from the leader or from each other. Most of this will operate below the level of what can be spoken. So, for instance, in any group there will be tacit 'rules', known and accepted by every member, even if the 'rule' is 'we don't have rules'. Common rules might include:

- It's important to stick to our routines.
- Everyone must have a little bit of their own way.
- Our meetings are deadly dull but it's not possible to challenge the Chair.
- We must all say at all times how fond we are of each other.

The more such rules are about fear, the more restrictive they are likely to be. As the family therapists like to point out, a family in trouble will have rigid rules that can never be discussed. A healthy family surfaces its rules and makes them constantly open to renegotiation.

The most brilliant fictional representation of this process is William Golding's allegorical book *Lord of the Flies*, first published in 1954, when the deadly dangers of the Cold War were becoming apparent. It is a book with a profoundly pessimistic view of human nature. A group of British schoolboys are marooned on a desert island after what we assume has been a nuclear war. No adults have survived and the boys quickly descend into savagery. Their overt task is to be rescued but their efforts to light a signal fire and indeed to survive at all are constantly sabotaged by their raw terror. Their superstitious dread of The Beast (in reality the corpse of an airman), their brutal fights over leadership, the murder of scapegoats, the emergence of pairs and factions is a perfect representation of what can happen when the primitive emotions of the basic assumption group are acted out in circumstances where there is no social control.

Projection

The assumption is that we all have dark sides that we may not acknowledge about ourselves. We say to ourselves, in effect, 'I don't like this about myself. I'll project it on to someone else and that way I can criticize it because then it's nothing to do with me'. The phenomenon of projection may take a number of forms.

At its simplest, we may project an emotion we are feeling onto someone else. This is because we cannot or will not own the feeling in ourselves. So, for instance, I might say to a friend, 'You seem worried', when actually it is I who am worried, but do not want to face my worry. As a facilitator, you might start thinking, 'This group is hostile to me', when in fact, you are feeling hostility towards them. When we criticize other people, what we criticize may be the very thing we most fear could be true about ourselves. You will also see projection at work in the group you are facilitating. Using Bion's framework, you will for instance see group members project unrealistic hopes of rescue onto leaders, temporarily endowing them with the skills or personality that group members would love to have themselves.

Transference and counter-transference

Transference means that group members unconsciously project onto you or each other patterns and assumptions from earlier relationships in their lives. These projections will be distortions – they are preventing the other person from seeing you as you think you really are. So group members may transfer feelings they still have to their bosses about authority figures from their past. A participant who constantly rebelled against an authoritarian father may see some male figures such as their manager in the same light as he saw his father, even though the boss concerned is a mild and pleasant person who is totally unlike the father. You will also be the focus of the same phenomenon from participants. For instance, as an older woman, I am conscious that I may create expectations of being a mother or a teacher to a participant and that this could trigger both rebellious adolescent behaviour and expectations of being nurtured.

Transference may be positive or negative. Where it is positive, participants may unconsciously associate you or another group member with a loved figure from their past, and this may be a useful temporary way to help the learning get going. More commonly, transference will be negative and comes from unrecognized distress and pain in the person's past. The object of the transference becomes the target and scapegoat for all the hurt which that person has experienced. To this extent, transference is an unaware defence against dealing with the original and persisting distress. The phenomenon of stalking is probably an extreme example of this process at work.

When you are the target of negative transference, this can be painful, not least because it takes you by surprise and feels outrageously unfair. Counter-transference may also be going on; that is, when you as facilitator do the same onto the group member. So a challenge from a group member may reawaken ghosts from an early relationship. For that moment, the participant is standing in for the ghost and you respond as you might have to him or her in the past. This is one more reason why as a facilitator you need to be acutely self-aware. All your own personal issues and anxieties need to be left well outside the process of facilitating. If you ever find yourself taking an intense and unreasonable dislike to one particular participant – beware! Similarly, remember that these phenomena could be affecting each and every member of the group in their relationships with each other, as well as in their relationships with you.

Transactional analysis

Transactional analysis (TA) originated in the 1960s with the gifted psychoanalyst Eric Berne, author of the best-selling book *Games People Play* (1968). To some extent TA has become the victim of its own success, with concepts such as assertiveness, 'win-win', 'games-playing' and 'I'm OK, you're OK' passing into popular consciousness without people necessarily knowing their origin. Berne's philosophy was that each of us has the right to have our needs met and getting to our full potential as human beings. TA is profoundly committed to the value of mutual respect as a means of human interaction. In their excellent book on TA, Ian Stewart and Vann Joines (1987) define it as 'a theory of personality and a systematic psychotherapy of personal growth and personal change'.

TA describes three roles or 'ego states' that it says we are all in at any given point: parent, adult and child. All are based on our early experience. As parent we judge and tell. The way we do this will depend on how we saw this done when we were children. The parent state has two variants: Controlling Parent that is full of precepts and rules – do this, don't do that, shoulds and shouldn'ts; Nurturing Parent protects, advises and guides. So when as facilitator you are in Parent state, you are taking responsibility for the group, either by providing rules ('We'll take a break now'; 'I don't think it's appropriate to discuss that now, X') or by providing comfort and advice ('I noticed you were upset when we discussed that incident – can I help in any way?'). Both these states may be useful at various stages with a group. Controlling Parent may be especially useful at the early stages of group life, and nurturing parent will help make it clear that the group is a safe place to be. The more malign version of Controlling Parent – bossy, judgemental and rigid is never useful as a facilitator.

Adult state is unemotional and detached. It is based on what is happening in the here and now. It uses rationality and logic. It is the state we are in when we are problem-solving. There is no assumption that the Adult state is the 'best' state to be in. When you are facilitating in Adult state, you will be relaxed, calm, friendly and slightly detached.

Child state has two variants. Adapted Child is the one we adopt when we feel dependent, apologetic, anxious and insecure. We expect to be told what to do at the same time as sulkily rebelling against it. Adapted Child is an unhelpful facilitator state because it is associated with lack of confidence and inability to stand up for yourself except to complain or rebel. Natural Child is the one where we feel gloriously free to be creative, to have fun. It can be a useful role for a facilitator when a group needs encouragement to be creative and spontaneous.

The transactional part of TA is important because it suggests that our ego states interact with the ego states of others, calling forth predictable responses. So, for instance, if you have a group that is stuck for some reason in a collective Adapted Child state, producing surly and uncooperative behaviour, the danger will be of 'hooking' your Controlling Parent where you reproach them or tell them to pull themselves together. On the other hand, if you want to use Natural Child when your group wants to stay in Adult, then you might also have trouble. If you are operating in Adult state, then you may produce a matching Adult state from the group – and so on.

The drama triangle

TA offers us the concept of 'games' – unhealthy patterns of interaction that can seem like games because they operate according to rules that all the 'players' understand perfectly, but which are never stated openly and never resolved. Think of any argument you have frequently and recurrently with any important person in your life and the chances are that a game will be at work. An obvious example is the 'game' most parents have played with their children.

> It's time to go to bed.
>
> *Just let me stay up for the end of this programme.*

> It's time to go to bed.
>
> *She/he (younger/older sibling) doesn't have to, why should I?*

> Adults need time for themselves so get to bed now!
>
> *You said I could stay up sometimes.*

Games are always a way of justifying emotion that would otherwise require us to take an adult level of responsibility for our own feelings. The choice to play them is made at an unconscious level. By definition a game never resolves the discomfort of the underlying feelings but allows us to luxuriate in anger, self-righteousness or self-pity.

In the Drama Triangle, an idea first developed by Stephen Karpman (1968) there are three roles:

1   *Victim: it's all terrible, whatever I do is wrong; I am helpless; others – or the system – are always against me.* The victim role is essentially manipulative. Its purpose is to force others to be responsible for the

victim's happiness: something that is literally impossible. No one can make another person happy or unhappy.

2   *Persecutor: I have the power, it's my right to tell you what to do; you are inferior.* The persecutor role is about win–lose. You have to be right at all costs; decisions are black or white, there are no shades of grey. People are either on your side or totally against you.

3   *Rescuer: It's my role to be the helper; I care about you; I can come to your aid.* Rescuing is underpinned by pity and disrespect based on the patronizing assumption that the person you are rescuing cannot make choices for themselves. Rescuing is always about the rescuer's needs, not the victim's. When we are in rescuing mode we need the dependency that the victim provides. 'They can't function without me.'

The point about the Drama Triangle in Figure 2.1 is that these are all distress-driven roles. Each 'player' is acting in order to get their own unconscious needs met. Each of the three roles has a healthy version. Leader is the healthy version of persecutor, follower is the healthy version of victim and colleague-collaborator is the healthy version of rescuer. The Drama Triangle is a dynamic model because the players constantly shift roles. So when rescuers try to rescue, victims may turn on them complaining that their rescuing is not helpful enough, thus becoming persecutors. Or persecutors, if attacked by rescuers for bullying, may collapse in self-pity complaining that they are only doing

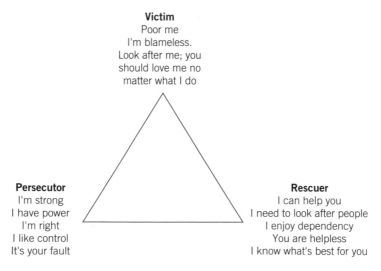

Figure 2.1   The drama triangle

their best to provide direction and no one appreciates them, thus becoming victims, making rescuers now persecutors. Feeling guilty, the previous victim now tries a little rescuing, comforting the new victim. The Drama Triangle is seductive: the players are self-absorbed, unable to think beyond their own needs. The false sense of excitement the game generates distracts them from the real issues and therefore from solving their problems. The payoff is the short-term reward that this excitement generates and the refuge it seems to supply from dealing with the underlying issues. The Drama Triangle is about avoiding intimacy – the crisis of the game provides an intensity that should be present in the relationships themselves but is avoided out of fear. There are no winners in the Drama Triangle. In fact, it would be common for people who typically play persecutor and rescuer to say they feel like victims themselves.

A colleague specializing in the healthcare sector describes this example:

> The scenario: three of the top people in a Primary Care Trust: the Chief Executive, The Chair and the doctor representative of the General Practitioners. In individual private meetings, all took the victim posture, telling me that each of the others was the persecutor. The GP also told me that he saw his role as keeping the peace (rescuer) because this was really 'just a cat-fight' – i.e. it could be explained by the fact that the other two were women. At the first meeting of all four of us I saw how relentlessly they cycled between the three drama triangle roles. The Chair would express helplessness about having any impact on the organisation, saying she was only paid to do so many days per week and the money was a pittance anyway (victim). The GP would then imply that the Chair's role was pointless, imposed on them by the government and that he couldn't see how she added value (persecutor) because all the important decisions should be made by doctors. The Chief Executive would then be rescuer, saying that she felt that the Chair was a valuable and necessary buffer, then would turn on the doctor to accuse him of stirring up the GPs against her (persecutor). The doctor then became the victim, complaining that managers in the NHS never, ever, understood clinicians but that without clinicians what would the NHS be? I am compressing here: all of this was wrapped up in hours of circumlocution and faux-politeness. The discussion had a kind of horrible vigour and energy – at some level, they loved it while also professing despair at its negativity.

Groupthink

The word 'groupthink' was coined by the writer William Whyte in 1952 but it was given further depth by Irving Janis (1982). We have all been members of such groups. Poor quality decisions are made but we suppress our unease. Alternatively, we cling to the idea that everything will turn out all right because we are special so we denigrate critics as people who do not understand and are therefore inferiors. We grumble outside the meetings maybe with people we perceive to share our views, but only in private. If events later prove that the decision we silently endorsed was, indeed, flawed, we do then express our dissent, most probably sulkily and angrily, saying we always knew it would turn out badly. We may be challenged by others in the group: *what prevented you speaking up?* The defensive answer will always be that we did not believe we would have been heard or else had lost personal confidence, believing that others genuinely knew best. Groupthink is one of the main characteristics of dysfunctional groups, whether at the extreme of cults such as the Unification Church or at the everyday discomfort of a board of governors' meeting at your local school. As a facilitator, you will meet groupthink repeatedly and one of your main roles will be to challenge it.

Symptoms of groupthink

To challenge it, you need to recognize the symptoms of groupthink. Janis identified eight:

1   Illusions of invulnerability that create a high level of optimism and therefore encourage unwise risk-taking.
2   Rationalizing warnings that might otherwise challenge the group's assumptions.
3   Unquestioned belief in the moral rightness of the group's *raison d'être* so whatever happens later can apparently be justified on moral grounds.
4   Stereotyping opponents as inferior beings who do not deserve respect.
5   Direct pressure to conform. If you challenge, then you are accused of being disloyal.
6   Self-censorship: consciously editing out opinions that would deviate from the prevailing consensus.
7   Illusions of unanimity: if you are silent, the assumption is that you agree.
8   Mindguards: members who see their self-selected role as being to

protect the group from any information that would challenge the apparent consensus.

You do not have to look far to see the pervasiveness of groupthink in public life. The disastrous consequences of the Iraq War were never predicted by the Bush administration, in the grip as they were in 2003, of their shared beliefs: in 'shock and awe' tactics (impregnability) and therefore that the war would be over in a few days; the moral rightness and superiority of the US way of life (why wouldn't everyone want some of that?); dismissing the astonishing level of angry street protest all over the world as *leftie conspiracy*; stereotyping Iraqis as patsies who would either welcome the invaders or just feebly cave in; rejecting the clear warnings of the UN inspectors that there most probably were no weapons of mass destruction (mindguards and self-censorship). The mistakes of the Bush Cabinet were mirrored by matching groupthink in the intelligence community. Similarly, the profoundly shaken belief of British voters in 2009–10 in our whole political system was caused by the groupthink of members of parliament who had padded their unrealistically modest salaries with an elaborate system of generous allowances. Inside the closed culture of Westminster, many MPs seem genuinely to have believed that they were entitled to openly bizarre and extreme versions of these allowances. Self-regulation ensured that the Fees Office, supposedly the guardian of the taxpayers' interests, became a way of bending the rules (institutionalized mindguards). When the story finally broke, the House and its officers still claimed that MPs were entitled to special treatment (rationalizing challenges to assumptions). Their collective shock shows how far the illusions of invulnerability had penetrated: it clearly had never occurred to most of them to ask, *What would this look like if it came out?* Even in their bleats of protest when exposed, you can see how far groupthink had penetrated: *I thought it was all right because everyone was doing it* (illusions of unanimity); *I was entitled to it because MPs aren't paid enough* (unquestioned belief in the morality of their actions); *the people who criticize me are just jealous, they're little people; how dare you intervene in my private affairs?* (stereotyping opponents as weak, spiteful, inferior).

The Abilene paradox

Other writers and researchers have shown how groupthink happens. For instance, Jerry Harvey (1988) a US academic who writes with a rare combination of wisdom, candour and ability to entertain, invented the term *the Abilene paradox*. He describes sitting with his family on a hot day in Texas when someone suggests driving to Abilene, a good 50 miles away, to lunch in a restaurant. Everyone agrees. The journey is hot and uncomfortable, the meal indifferent, but no one says so. Making polite conversation back at home, Jerry comments, privately squirming at his own inauthenticity, on how good the meal and trip had been. Slowly, one by one, everyone confesses that they had never wanted to go and had disliked the whole affair. This is the paradox of Abilene: everyone agrees to do what nobody really wants to do: a phenomenon that it is your bounden duty as a facilitator to challenge every time you see it – which will be often.

The Stanford experiment

In a notorious and fascinating experiment in the early 1970s, Philip Zimbardo, a professor of psychology, turned a bland part of the Stanford University campus into a 'prison', recruiting a cohort of psychologically stable young men to become 'prisoners' and 'guards'. The roles were randomly assigned. Within a short time, as groupthink set in, the 'guards' were enthusiastically abusing and humiliating their 'prisoners', putting paper bags over their heads, making them clean lavatories with their bare hands and forcing conformity from colleagues who dared to suggest that what they were doing was morally wrong. Zimbardo himself, enchanted by the dramatic turn of events, was also in the grip of a form of groupthink. The experiment was stopped only when his fiancée and colleague arrived on its fifth day and was appalled at what was going on, ordering them to stop on the grounds that it was unethical. Both Zimbardo and the 'guards' put up fierce resistance to her challenge.[2]

The Asch experiments

Solomon Asch (1951) ran a series of experiments where naïve subjects were recruited to take part in what they thought were tests of visual acuity. The group was given a card with three vertical lines on it side by side and then a second card with one vertical line. The supposed task was to say which of the lines on the first card was identical to the line on the second. Unknown to the naïve subject, the group was rigged to endorse an incorrect answer. Despite the clear evidence of their own eyes, a third of the subjects agreed with the obviously wrong answer. Many of them later blamed their glasses or trouble with their eyes as an explanation. The real culprit was an artificially induced groupthink, where, interestingly, there was no overt pressure to agree.

How does groupthink develop?

Janis suggested that groupthink flourishes where for whatever reason a group is isolated from the challenges that would otherwise pierce its defences. For instance, in an organization an executive team may be geographically isolated: I can think of many client teams that have exclusively inhabited a different floor, eating together in a directors' dining room, parking their cars in special places, travelling first class and sometimes having offices in a building that is totally separate from the organization they lead. Where its members share similar backgrounds, attitudes, education and career histories, again as is true of many executive teams, their insulation can become isolation. Where this is combined with a directive style of leadership plus an apparently high level of external threat with a complex set of moral or physical challenges, groupthink can set in.

Janis analysed the mental habits in which groupthink flourishes:

- incomplete appraisal of alternatives to decisions and information
- incomplete appraisal of objectives
- failing to evaluate the possible risks of decisions
- not re-examining alternatives that had previously been rejected
- lack of thorough data search
- bias in selecting the information on which decisions are made
- failing to establish contingency plans

You will realize at once that all these mental habits are critical areas for facilitators. First you must notice them. Then your design toolkit must contain multiple ways of allowing groups to expand their thinking. Just to take some simple examples, tools such as SWOT (p. 75) oblige a team to look its threats and weaknesses in the eye. Decision-making tools (p. 92) help guard against the tendency to close options down too soon. Large group interventions (p. 98) are expressly designed to bring a wide range of opinions into the equation. The essence of groupthink is that dissent becomes impossible. Opinions that look likely to be unpopular are suppressed, often through self-censorship. Noticing the tiny signs of this – a fleeting frown, a prolonged silence, a look of discomfort – allows you as facilitator to invite the dissenter to speak.

As a facilitator you will most probably only be brought in when the disastrous consequences of groupthink, personal and organizational, are becoming apparent. This colleague describes such a scenario:

> An executive team called me in for some so-called 'teambuilding' in the uncertainty created while they awaited the appointment of a new boss. Their previous Chief Executive had presided over a financial disaster. It was striking that the team appeared so similar. They were all tall dark men of roughly the same age, long-stayers in the organisation with similar social origins and leisure interests and all graduates of the same two universities. Junior people in the organisation had attempted to bring them bad news but had been brushed off as 'stupid pessimists'. By the time I worked with them they were blaming each

other and bewildered by the speed of decline. Our discussions quickly showed that testing ideas in rigorous discussion was seen as disloyalty or 'not being corporate'. Juniors presenting paper at their meetings commonly described 'Being Star-Chambered' because the reception was invariably hostile unless it endorsed an existing plan. I thought it unlikely that many of them would survive the eventual arrival of the new CEO: of different nationality, with a different career history – and a woman!

Cycles of group life

Tuckman and Jensen's framework

This well-known framework for understanding groups was suggested by Tuckman and Jensen (Tuckman, 1965). It offers a simple, logical approach to understanding group life:

Forming → Storming → Norming → Performing

Forming

The Forming phase is about the uncertainty group members feel at the beginning of the group's life. There is anxiety and also a degree of pleasant anticipation. There is a sense of looking to the leader to provide direction and safety. At this phase a false consensus often develops. We make assumptions that our own beliefs and values and purposes are just like those of others. Other people may politely remain silent if they disagree with such assertions.

As a facilitator, there is a major responsibility on you at this phase: the group is looking to you to model the behaviour that says, 'It's safe to be here, this occasion does have a purpose'.

Storming

In the Storming phase, naked conflict may develop. As a facilitator, you may be challenged openly with requests to clarify 'what all this is about' or 'why we're here'. Such challenges may upset other members of the group who in their turn challenge the challengers. This phase is unsettling to group members. They are torn between their wish to make the group what they want it to be and their fear of punishment from the facilitator or other members of the group.

Norming

The Norming phase is about the emergence of tacit or openly stated rules about how the group is to be. The group now knows one another better and has begun to settle down. Subgroups may have formed and people know who their kindred spirits are. The fragile consensus of the Forming stage has disappeared and there is a lot less dependence on the facilitator. The norms may or may not be helpful. For instance, if the group decides that one of its norms is that it will have a jolly good time and also refuses to be serious, that may have implications for the quality of its work.

Performing
Performing is the stage where the group buckles down to its task. How well this is done will depend on what norms have been established at the earlier phases. The group becomes conscious of its deadlines and will agree roles.

Mourning
This phase was added to the framework later. Mourning is about how the group copes with disbandment. A group that has become close may view the ending of its life with dismay. You can help people cope with this phase by having some sort of closing ceremony. This does not have to be so tooth-gratingly sentimental as it was on a course I attended in the USA where we were exhorted to hold hands in a big circle singing along to a tape. At the simplest level it is helpful just to look back over what has been achieved and to look forward to how the lessons are going to be applied.

Inclusion, control and affection: Will Schutz's ideas

There are many other useful frameworks for understanding what is happening in a group. A particularly valuable one was developed by Will Schutz (1958) the originator of the FIRO-B™, a well-known psychometric questionnaire.

Schutz offers the idea that our relationships with each other and in groups are governed by three interpersonal needs. He called these Inclusion, Control and Affection. There is a wide spectrum of legitimate needs on all three.

Inclusion is about the need for both giving and receiving recognition as part of a group. It is about wanting just the right amount of contact with other people. Some people may want a great deal, others are happy with a modest amount of contact and may typically be choosy about how and when they associate with others. Inclusion resembles Tuckman's Forming stage.

Control is about how much influence, structure and leadership you need to express, as well as how much you want to be influenced by others. For instance, you may feel you want to be in charge of everything but do not want to be greatly influenced by other people. Or you may feel you work best within a structured environment where it is clear who is in charge, while not wanting to take a dominant role yourself. Control resembles Tuckman's Storming phase.

Affection is about how much closeness you are prepared to give to and want from others. Some people like to express affection openly to a great many people; others prefer to keep a distance except with a chosen few. Some people give little overt affection but want a great deal from others. Affection has some resemblance to Tuckman's Norming and Performing phases, as both are about the emergence of trust in the group.

Schutz suggests that these principles operate in all of us as individuals, but they also apply to the life of a group. Where issues concerning Inclusion, Control and Affection are not acknowledged and resolved, Schutz suggests that there will be 'negative energy'; in other words, emotional energy will leach into areas that absorb the group in ways that are not helpful to its task or process.

Stage 1   Inclusion – am I in or out of this group?
In its earliest stages, group members are most concerned with issues such as:

- Do I want to belong to this group?
- Are these people going to like me?
- Will I be recognized as a significant and valuable person here?
- Is this the kind of group where I can feel at home?

This stage is accompanied by the exchange of apparently trivial information: where you live, what your job is, your views on the weather and so on. Some questions to ask about the Inclusion phase of a new group would be:

- Does the group make it easy for new members to be accepted?
- Does the group socialize outside its actual meetings?
- Do people frequently give each other feedback?
- Is it possible to tell that people belong to this group by what they wear, how they work or what they do?
- Is it important for people to say that they are part of this group?
- Do people have fun or are things always serious?

When a group has not dealt with Inclusion issues, you may see the following signs of trouble:

- people arriving late and leaving early
- absenteeism
- presenteeism (i.e. physically present but mentally absent, daydreaming, writing notes or working on 'real' work not relevant to the group's concerns)
- one or more people seeking prominence, for example, over-contributing in order to seek recognition from other members of the group

- under-contributing from a number of people
- cliques and factions
- information being restricted
- little emphasis on celebration or socializing

As a facilitator, your aim should be to acknowledge the discomforts of the Inclusion phase and to help participants through it as soon as possible. This is why ice-breakers (see p. 71) are so important – they help people to feel, 'Yes, I really am here' and to commit to the group.

Remember that the same rules of human behaviour apply to you as they do to the group. You, too, will be affected by Inclusion anxieties. 'Do I like these people? Do I want to be part of this group? Will they accept me?' This anxiety can be particularly acute when you are working with a group that already knows each other well and you are the stranger. It is their group and you are joining it. This can easily induce feelings of being the unwelcome outsider.

Stage 2   Control: who is in charge?
When the inclusion issues are resolved, Schutz suggests that the group becomes preoccupied with who is going to control the group. Who are the influential people? Who decides what the rules are? Who sets the standards? What happens if someone makes a mistake? This stage may see several people struggling for leadership, for instance, through fierce arguments and possibly challenging you as the facilitator.

Some questions to ask about the Control phase of a group would be:

- Who is leading the group? Is the real leader the same as the official leader?
- Who has influence in the group? How is this influence expressed?
- What norms have emerged in the group; for example, about who speaks when?
- Who decides when the group will have breaks and all the other issues to do with how the time is managed?
- When conflict breaks out, what is it about? Who manages it?
- How much structure is there and how much is just going with the flow?

When the Control issues have not been dealt with in a group, you may expect to see the following signs of trouble:

- Open rebellion – 'We've been discussing this and we don't want to do x or y thing'.

- Covert rebellion – sabotage; mute protest (e.g. not doing tasks agreed between meetings); sulking.
- Competitiveness – who's the best at this or that?
- Struggles for leadership.
- Status consciousness.
- Overemphasis on rules and regulations; attempts to stop people doing things.
- The real decisions being taken in subgroups away from the group's official meetings.
- Expressed concerns with competence and standards (e.g. anxiety that other groups are performing 'better').
- Blaming and scapegoating.

The facilitator's role is vital here as at both the other phases. Expect that there will be some Control issues and be ready for them. Hone your conflict-management skills and be clear how comfortable you are with your own leadership style.

Stage 3   *Affection: how much do we trust and like each other?*
When the leadership issues are settled, the group moves on to Affection. This is about how much closeness or distance is permissible and wanted in the group. Affection is about relationships between pairs. In a group where there is a high level of affection, there will be a multiplicity of such relationships in the group. The issues here concern:

- Is it safe to disclose how I really feel here?
- Can I trust the confidentiality of this group?
- Will people support me?
- Is it all right to develop a real friendship here or are these just superficial professional relationships that don't really matter?
- How much real openness is there?

When Affection issues have not been dealt with in a group you would expect to see the following signs of trouble:

- lack of trust
- refusal to disclose anything personal; the group's relationships with each other are superficial
- jealousy and suspicion
- conflict being suppressed inside the group's meetings but discussed outside them
- a cool detached atmosphere

- sexual or racial issues surfacing (e.g. as rivalry, accusations of abuse or harassment; overemphasis on being politically correct)

You will have set the tone for the Affection phase through your own earlier behaviour in the group, especially in its Inclusion phase. The sooner you are able to create an open atmosphere where there is trust and liking, the more quickly the group will be able to operate in affection mode.

Schutz suggests that the whole process is dynamic. It happens in the order described above (i.e. Inclusion, Control and Affection) but it also cycles continuously (see Figure 2.2). So, for instance, if someone leaves or joins a group, this will immediately recreate emphasis on Inclusion; a new task will reopen Control issues and so on.

The closing phases

When a group is going to disband, Schutz says that the process happens again but in the reverse order. So in the early stages of disbandment, people begin to withdraw from rapport with each other (the Affection phase). Next comes the Control phase when people focus on leaders and their wish to go along with or to rebel against their desires. Finally, people work through the Inclusion issues by talking about whether or not the group can continue its existence in any way. Often people will begin to mention the other groups and tasks that will begin to claim or reclaim their time and attention.

Relationships in the group

This part of group life is about the quality of relationships between members, and between them and you. It is easy to overlook how many such relationships there are between group members. So in a group of 11 plus yourself, for

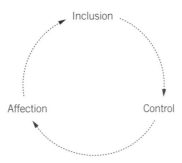

Figure 2.2 Will Schutz cycle of group life

instance, there will be 66 different relationships possible. This is the number you obtain when you do the following sum:

$$\frac{\text{Number in the group} \times \text{number in group} - 1}{2}$$

So $12 \times 11 \div 2 = 66$

Replaying family dynamics

For all of us, our primary experiences of being in a group were formed as children in a family. Our main responses to authority, and our typical responses to the feelings of dependency this created, were probably set here. Being in a group can reawaken such feelings at an unconscious level. One way of thinking about the group you are facilitating is therefore to think of it as being like a family. The participants may sometimes behave as rival siblings, each perhaps wanting to be the cleverest, the nicest, the most loved. Former family roles may also be replayed in the group: family clown, responsible eldest child, naughty child. You may see behaviour in the group that shows you that this may be what is going on; for instance, the person who constantly bids for attention, the one who is a 'little mother' to others in the group, the silent observer who likes to be watching from the outside, the sulky rebel who never wants to join in. Your personal experiences will have affected your own attitudes to power and dependency and will have had a radical effect on your feelings of comfort or discomfort with the facilitator and leadership role. Do you, for instance, want to be 'one of the gang' with the group as a way of recreating the feelings of us against them that you had with your siblings against your parents? Do you, perhaps, relish the feeling of power that the facilitator role gives you because in that way you recreate the enjoyable feeling of being the trusted and responsible eldest? Do you like to transfer power to the group as quickly as possible because that feels comfortable in the same way that it did when you were the carefree youngest in the family?

Informal roles

The work of Meredith Belbin (2004) is well known in the UK for the insight it gives into informal roles in groups. Belbin's work in the early 1970s at the Henley Management College set out with the assumption that the most effective group would be the one whose members had the highest collective IQ. Groups of management students were asked to play a version of Monopoly called Teamopoly. This version required the teams to bargain with each other thus preventing the early emergence of one dominant player that you typically see in Monopoly. Contrary to expectation, the 'clever' groups almost invariably came last. Belbin identified eight, later nine, informal roles in groups and his assumption is that an effective group needs to have at least four of his roles played. Although it is not a theory of personality, Belbin does assert that most of us have roles that we prefer to play and that these will tend to be consistent over time.

Belbin's informal roles define a strength for each role and also an 'allowable weakness'. The roles are:

- *Shaper*: the dynamo for the task can be aggressive.
- *Plant*: the ideas person who can also be too head in the clouds for reality.
- *Resource investigator*: the extroverted person who always knows the latest ideas and someone who can help, but gets bored easily.
- *Coordinator*: the person who can combine persuasiveness with concentration on the task, though may not be as intellectually gifted as the Plant.
- *Teamworker*: bridge-builder and comforter, but may find tough decisions difficult.
- *Completer-finisher*: the detail-conscious person who worries away at making sure things are done but may lose sight of the bigger picture.
- *Implementer*: makes sure that things happen but may lack inspiration and flexibility.
- *Monitor-evaluator*: the solid strategic thinker who asks the tough 'yes but' questions but may seem dour and negative.
- *Specialist*: the person who has important but narrow expertise.

Belbin's framework makes for a useful group exercise. By taking the associated questionnaire (the original is copyright-free) you see which roles may be over- or under-represented in the group and how this may explain any difficulties it is encountering. For instance, an argumentative group may be full of Shapers, a group that likes discussing ideas but never turns them into action may have a dominance of Plants, and so on but may lack someone who delivers on the details (Completer-Finisher) or who has excellent networking skills (Resource Investigator).

Implications for facilitators

Explaining group behaviour

Understanding what makes groups tick will enable you to see that the seemingly puzzling behaviour of the group you are facilitating can make eminent sense when put against the template of certain theories. It can give you heart when you begin to think that it is solely your responsibility if something apparently goes dramatically wrong. This is not an excuse for any of your own shortcomings, but it does help guard against unnecessary self-flagellation. Group behaviour is not random: much of the time it is predictable. So, for instance, if you know that the threat of disintegration is one of the elements that keeps the group together at the same time as the need for autonomy drives the individuals apart, it can explain what can otherwise look like childish outbursts from group members. Most of the apparently nightmare scenarios described in Chapter 6 can be explained this way.

Using the frameworks with the group

These ideas are too useful to keep to yourself. In the right circumstances they can also be shared with the group or with individuals in it. A colleague and I worked with an executive team that had been the focus of bitter complaints about the quality of its in-house customer services. As we got to know this team through a regular series of off-site meetings, we noticed that in the intervening periods, there was always someone who had become the focus of the group's hostility. First X was the problem because of his alleged 'extreme introversion', then it was Y who never 'delivered' on his part of the business, then it was Z who apparently allowed 'sloppy work' to get through. We challenged this team, briefly describing the theory and naming the phenomenon 'Scapegoat of the Month' and spent a good half day unpeeling the dynamics that lay behind it. The group bravely concluded that in effect they were projecting their own fears onto the scapegoated colleagues. These fears were about the difficulty of moving quickly enough to provide the higher-quality service their customers were demanding while simultaneously containing rising costs. Underneath this worry, there was the deeper concern about whether their department could survive. Would the host organization become impatient? Would it all be outsourced? Would they lose their jobs? The 'scapegoat' discussion was a turning point in our work with this team, allowing much that had been hidden to be surfaced, named, and therefore diminished in its destructive power, allowing attention to focus at last on the tough topic of how to redesign the business to meet the needs of its customers.

Self-awareness

There are lesson for self-awareness in these ideas. You will be as affected by all the phenomena described here as any of the group members with whom you are working. It is not possible to have a 'neutral' style. When you are facilitating you will always be doing one style or another, whether you are aware of it or not.

As a facilitator you are a leader of sorts, so the psychoanalytical perspective on leadership and the ambivalent feelings of dependency it creates will apply to you as much as to the leader of any group with whom you are working. You should expect any of the typical reactions to your leadership that Bion and others suggested, described earlier in this chapter. Examples of what may be going on for group members at the level of magical thinking may include those listed in Table 2.1.

You (the facilitator) are in charge	*so*	I will rely on you and avoid responsibility for myself or others
You are clever	*so*	I can be stupid
You will take care of me	*so*	I don't have to take care of myself and in return I will offer you adoration
You are all-powerful	*so*	I must have your approval and affection
You are absolutely obliged to be perfect	*so*	Don't disappoint me: I will point out any imperfection under the guise of 'feedback' until you beg for forgiveness

Table 2.1

This may in turn set up a matching set of behaviours from you (see Table 2.2). The lesson here is: do not get sucked into this. Notice it, challenge it. Some ways to do this are the focus of Chapters 5 and 6.

If I (facilitator) have to be perfect	*then*	I can't admit to any weakness or show vulnerability
If you need my approval	*then*	I can never show disapproval of your behaviour
If I have to be in charge the whole time	*then*	I must make all the decisions and wear myself out in doing so – it goes with the patch
If only my affection is good enough for you	*then*	I must be like a mother-hen and protect you from yourself and others

Table 2.2

Facilitation as a continuum

As a facilitator-leader you have choices about the style you employ. All may have something to recommend them, depending on the circumstances: you, the group, the task and the environment. There is no better than or worse than style, but all styles have consequences, pluses and minuses.

The underlying framework is the familiar one suggested by Tannenbaum and Schmidt (1958) in a famous *Harvard Business Review* article. They suggested a graph of leadership styles: the more power you, as leader, have, the less power the 'led' (the group) have, and vice versa.

What applies to leadership in organizations applies to facilitators in groups. This is because facilitating a group involves the use of power and influence – either by you or by the group or by some blend of the two. For instance, think about all the topics on which someone has to make decisions:

- Purpose – why are we here?
- How do we manage: the time, the venue, the breaks, the food?
- What subjects should we be talking about?
- How will we structure them?
- Group together: how will we behave when we are together?
- Group apart: how will we communicate? If we have tasks to complete between meetings, who will do them?
- Leadership: who is really in charge?

This is not meant to be an exhaustive list. However, even just looking at this list, it shows the possibilities for conflict, confusion and error. So, inside the possibly simplistic-looking Tannenbaum and Schmidt framework, there is a lot of room for subtlety. Consciously or unconsciously, you and your group will be negotiating around these topics continuously. It is a dynamic process – never settled or decided.

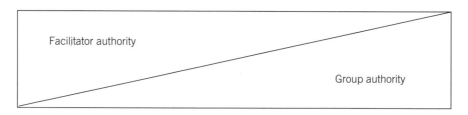

Figure 2.3 The authority spectrum

Facilitator style	1. Tells	2. Consults	3. Involves	4. Steps out
What happens	Facilitator is in charge of task and process: chooses venue; chooses agenda; chairs and leads discussion; prescribes; gives information; manages the time	Facilitator constantly consults the group on its needs Facilitates reconsideration and response to agenda issues Emphasizes consideration of group's needs May share leadership with some of the group	Group chooses how it will use facilitator skills Group may rotate leadership, decide to change agenda, timings and so on Facilitator still likely to feel responsible for group process	Group manages itself Facilitator becomes a resource to the group Facilitator may leave Group entirely responsible for its own process and task
Dominant state of group	Dependency	Submitting to benevolent government	Interdependence	Independence
Pluses	Group feels safe. Often right for early sessions while group settles down. May be very task-focused Facilitators may like it because it puts them in the expert-in-charge role	Gives group practice in taking responsibility for itself within safe framework; good compromise between the greater freedom of involvement and the bossier style of 'telling'	High performance; fun; purposeful atmosphere; exhilaration	Group cannot rebel as there is no authority figure; clear that group is totally responsible for own learning
Minuses	Group does not take responsibility for own learning; may 'rebel'; may feel childlike	Civilized dependency may be ultimately harmful; gloss of involvement is only skin deep; does not trust group to be adults; learning may be limited	Facilitators miss the old 'buzz' of being in charge; group gets worried by its own freedom; minimal involvement may look like abandonment or *laissez-faire*; takes time to get to this point and the group may not have this much time	Responsibility may be too much; group may fall apart without 'official' leadership; ambiguity may be too much for some members; control issues may surface again

Table 2.3

Conclusion

I would counsel against believing that you can or should interpret every interaction using any of the frameworks described here. They are vital background and help explain much that would otherwise be mystifying, but if you are too preoccupied with interpreting, you will miss much of what is actually in front of you. The old joke about interpretation says that it is 25 per cent right 25 per cent of the time; in other words, not often.

There is really just one overall theme in this chapter and it is a question. How are some of the big challenges of human interaction to be managed in the group? How will you cope with your own and the group's needs to resolve questions of recognition, dependency, power and sexuality? The models I offer here are just a beginning and it is important to say that they are models, no more, no less. As the Zen saying has it, 'The finger pointing at the moon is not the moon'.

Notes

1 www.human-nature.com/rmyoung.
2 The best account of this experiment is on the official website: www.prisonexp.org.

3   Preparation and design

If I had six hours to chop down a tree, I'd spend the first hour sharpening the ax.
(Abraham Lincoln, US President)

Luck favours the mind that is prepared.
(Louis Pasteur, scientist)

In advance

Many, possibly even most, of the problems that lie in wait to discomfit a facilitator are caused by lack of preparation, or the wrong kind of preparation. Here are some typical difficulties:

> The event never got off to a proper start. The participants seemed confused about my role. One asked another in a loud whisper, 'Who's that woman? What's she here for?'

> I was facilitating an event for a group working in music and the arts. I was challenged 30 minutes in by a participant who wanted to know by what right I was leading the discussion since I clearly knew nothing about opera.
> (Organization development consultants)

> It was supposedly a team-building day. After an hour I noticed some restlessness in the group. Two of the journalists spoke up. One said that he'd thought the meeting was going to end at lunchtime and he had a piece to write so couldn't stay. The other said he'd thought it was going to be about the relaunch of the sports segment.
> (Internal consultant, BBC)

My heart sank when I realised we'd got to the end of the morning and had still only dealt with two of the items on our long agenda. The choice then was, hurtle through the afternoon or openly confess to the client and renegotiate – in other words have the conversation we should have had in advance.

(Team coach)

Note: if you are reading this as a manager or meetings-chair, then you are your own client and should go direct to the section headed Designing: basic principles (p. 64).

The case for planning carefully

The purpose of investing time thoughtfully is to prevent any of these common problems occurring. Specifically, it is to uncover the answers to questions like these:

- Who is the real client?
- What are the underlying needs?
- Where are the 'elephants' (p. 8) and what are they?
- How is the culture of the organization likely to affect the outcomes of the event?
- Who in the group really has the power and influence?
- What might sabotage this event?
- Who must be there – and who should not be there?
- What is the true purpose of the event and how achievable is it given the resources available?
- Can I work with this client and group?

There are several stages that it is vital to go through, usefully described as 'the consulting cycle' (see Figure 3.1).

The consulting cycle

It is essential to pay attention to all its phases. The most common mistake made by inexperienced facilitators is to jump from phase 1, 'gaining entry' to phase 6, 'implementing'. When you do this it more or less guarantees failure. This chapter is about the first five phases of this cycle. 'Delivering' and 'evaluating' are the subjects of other chapters.

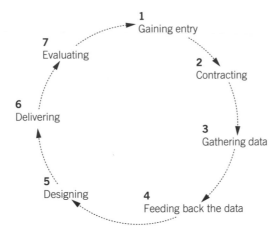

Figure 3.1   The seven stages of the consulting cycle

Phase 1 Gaining entry

> *Critical question: are you the right person for the job?*

The *gaining entry* phase is about establishing sufficient trust for the client to work with you and for you to feel that you have whatever the client needs. There are virtually always barriers to gaining entry. If you are an internal consultant your clients may believe that you lack the seniority to deal with their group. If you are an external consultant you may have to engage in a prolonged sales cycle where clients appear reluctant to hire you because you cost real money.

This phase is about establishing your credibility. You will do this by listening carefully to the client's concerns, talking judiciously about experience with other clients (but without betraying their confidentiality) and clarifying in outline that you are available and interested. Remember that you can refuse the assignment at this stage if it appears unlikely that you can meet the client's needs.

The gaining entry meeting will also help you establish who the real client is. The real client is the person who is footing any bills, who has the ultimate power to decide on the usefulness of the day and whether or not to implement any of its suggested outcomes. This is not necessarily the same as the person who initially contacts you. So your first question to yourself should always be, 'Am I talking to the real client?'

Phase 2 Contracting

> *Critical questions: Can we work together? Is what the client wants achievable with the resources available?*

The contracting meeting comes down to two main areas: task and relationship. Both are equally important. At the task level, the question is *What does the client want to get out of the event?* From your point of view, you will have a matching question, *What do I as a facilitator believe needs to happen during the event?*

At the relationship level, the question for both sides, not often put so bluntly as this, is 'Can we work together?'

Getting the task clear

Over the years I have been doing this work, I have come to rely on a few important questions for the client at this kind of meeting. If you ask these, you should find that they give you pricelessly valuable information:

> *What's the presenting issue here?*
>
> *What makes you feel that this event is essential?*
>
> *What makes it an issue right now?*

These questions give you some idea of what is on the client's mind, and will tell you what the symptoms are, not necessarily the underlying causes. The answers may be things such as, 'People don't get on very well here', or 'We need to agree a new strategy for x or y product', or 'This is a new team and we need to take some time to get to know each other'.

> *Let's suppose the event goes really well and this problem were solved. What would be happening? What evidence would you have that things were going really well?*

This question lifts the client out of the possible gloom of the answer to the first question by concentrating on the positive and gives you vital further information about the scope and depth of the issues.

> *What's preventing that ideal from happening now?*

The answers here will give you some idea of underlying causes of the problem – they may for instance show that other departments are involved, that people other than those who are going to be present on the day are also important.

What have you already tried?

It would be unusual for a client not to have tried many of the obvious solutions. Finding out what these have been will prevent you suggesting them and will invariably point you to the more serious underlying issues.

> *How might you (client) be contributing to this problem?* Alternative version of the question: *How are you getting in your own way here?*

It is axiomatic that all clients, however wonderfully well adapted they appear, will have contributed to the issue in some way, even if it is only through benign neglect. Asking this question, and surfacing the answer, prevents clients from believing that if only everyone else would change, life would be rosy. It is always useful for any of us to see that we are part of both the problem and the solution.

> *So how do you see the event I am going to be running for you helping to solve these problems?*

The answers here give you some idea of whether the client's hopes for the day are realistic or, as they often are, overambitious. For instance, it is highly unlikely that a team whose personal relationships are viciously antagonistic will end up wildly happy after a single event. If so, then a series of events is more likely to be productive, but the client may say that they can afford neither the time nor the money that this would involve.

> *What ideas do you have about what should definitely be in the day?*

Many clients have much experience of being facilitated and will have a shrewd idea of what will work and what will fail. Some may have favourite techniques that they have seen other facilitators use with success. Listen carefully and measure the client's ideas against your own judgement about what will work and what will not – including how you rate your own skill and familiarity with any particular techniques that are proposed.

> *Who should be present?*

The most appropriate answer may well have emerged through the replies to the earlier questions. Clients may want a huge number of people, far too many to be successfully facilitated by one person, or they may suggest a group that seems too small because so many of the people who have a stake in the outcome are not going to be there.

What do I need to know about the individuals who will be coming?

You will be talking to all these people yourself as part of your preparation (see 'Gathering data' opposite) but you also need your client's views on them. This is the place to establish from the client's perspective who might be challenging, who will be supportive and who might attempt sabotage.

Clarifying and building the relationship

Facilitating an event for clients mean that you share the power. You respect clients for their knowledge of the people and the issues. Clients respect you for your objectivity and expertise as a facilitator. So at the contracting meeting it will be important to discuss issues such as:

- Who makes the final decision on the design of the day?
- What reservations do you have about working with me or about the outcome of the day? (Clients always have some so it is better to get them said out loud.)
- How do you see my role?

At the same time as asking these questions of the client, you will have matters of your own that you will want to raise. The main ones are:

- What you expect from the client. These may be issues such as commenting on your draft design, booking the room, sending instructions about the venue, and briefing participants.
- What additional information you will want to gather, including interviewing participants.
- The boundaries of confidentiality.

Contracting traps

The main trap is of overpromising. If you really think it is impossible to cover everything the client wants, then the contracting meeting is the place and time to say so – not during or after the event, by which stage it will be far too late. If there is too little time, too little money, or both, then say so. It is rare for clients to hold out for everything they originally ask for when faced with respectful logic about how it is going to be impossible to deliver. For instance, if a manager asks you to facilitate a meeting where 30 people are going to be present, depending on the style of event, you may want to suggest that you need a co-facilitator and that this will cost money. The client may be reluctant to accept that this is necessary or may say that as much as they would like to do it, they do not have the budget. Your choices then are:

- Continue to make the case for the extra person and budget and hope that the client caves in.
- Ask if the client has anyone available internally who might make an acceptable extra facilitator.
- Rethink the design of the day so that you can do it alone competently.
- Subsidize the extra facilitator yourself or bring in a trainee as an unpaid helper.
- Wish client good luck and walk away.

The last option may feel like the most difficult, but sometimes it may be better than living with the feelings of dread associated with knowing that you cannot do good work on impossible terms.

There will also be issues about time-scales, fees, if any, and venues. The contracting meeting is the place to deal with them all. For instance, be clear about how important the venue is and surface any reservations about a venue you know to be shabby, noisy or uncomfortable. It is normally unwise, for instance, to hold an important awayday on site. People literally see things from the same old perspective, get distracted by thoughts of their emails and other allegedly important duties and find it difficult to give themselves wholly to the task in hand.

Phase 3 Gathering data

> *Critical questions at this stage: How can you acquire a reliable view of the issues as seen by the other participants? How can you build rapport with them? How far are the client's views shared?*

If you rely solely on your commissioning client's view of the issues, you risk creating severe problems on the day: people challenging your role and authority, telling you that you have missed the 'real' problems, acting out, seeing you as partial because the only person you have spoken to is the boss. As a minimum, aim to talk to a representative sample of the people who will be present. You need your client's active help to make this happen, fixing dates and times and alerting them to the contact. Ideally, talk to them all, assuming it is no more than a dozen people.

Interviews

You will need a minimum of 30 minutes with each person. If it is a large group then you can do the interviews in pairs or trios, but accept that you will get less candour. Make notes, but keep these to the main points. One of the other purposes of such interviews is to build rapport with participants, and you cannot do this if your head is in a notebook all the time. Again, there are a few questions that I have always found to be a useful core to such interviews with follow-up exploration on each one. Assure the person of non-attributable confidentiality; that is, you will not quote any individuals to the client or anyone else. Treat this promise seriously.

- Ask if they have any concerns about the interview and what they know about its purpose. Explain what the role of the facilitator is and what they will see you doing on the day.
- Ask about their role and history in the organization.

Now ask:

- What's going really well here? Ask for specific examples.
- What's not going so well? Ask for specific examples.
- If things were at their best, what would be happening?
- What's preventing things being at their best?
- If you could ask an oracle any two questions about the future, what would they be?
- What would having those answers do for you?
- If this team/group/organization played a sport or game, what would it be good at and bad at? Answers will tell you a great deal about how people see the group. For instance, a team whose members reply that they would be good at chess and bad at football will suggest that people see themselves as intellectual rivals and have difficulty cooperating.
- What are you hoping to get out of the day I will be facilitating for you?
- Is there anything else you would like to tell me? This last question is often the one that GPs call the handle-on-the-door question – the thing the patient has really wanted to say all along and can only muster courage to name at the last moment. Some necessary but uncomfortable truth is often blurted out at this stage.

Aim to include a verbal or written summary of their main themes on the day itself as well as feeding the themes back to your commissioner in advance of the event. Not only is this courteous for the people who have given you their time, but also most people are intensely curious to see where and how their own views fit in with those of others. The report itself is also a further stimulus to change.

Observation

Observation is a simple technique and often overlooked. This could involve you sitting in on meetings, shadowing the client or touring the client's area of operations. There are three issues with observation which you need to remember:

- your own biases
- your presence will alter whatever it is you are observing
- that it takes a very mature client to agree to the process

When you visit the client's premises, notice everything: what is on the walls, the state of the rooms, how you are greeted and treated. These things will have become invisible to the clients, but they are valuable data for you. Some years ago I was asked to meet a team at a small public sector organization to discuss a project. I arrived in plenty of time only to find that I could not actually get into the building. As I pressed a buzzer outside, I could clearly see a post-room and people working in it. They resolutely ignored me – one actually shrugged his shoulders. The building itself was in the middle of what appeared to be a traffic island and gave every appearance of being a gated community, earnestly devoted to repelling hostile outsiders, despite the stated commitment on their website to easy access for their user groups. Once at last inside the building I was left to find my own way via a labyrinthine route to the meeting room. This told me about their culture and some of their problems just as quickly and vividly as could have been achieved through conversation.

Secondary data

These are already existing records; for example, turnover, absenteeism, annual reports, grievances and minutes of meetings. Expect some bias as all organizations record data selectively. Access to records may also be a problem: ask for your client's help if you encounter blockages. Remember that there are no such things as objective data: all are filtered by the collecting agent, consciously or unconsciously. When a client encourages you to collect data prior to the event, in the end they are paying for your hunches, your experience and your developed intuition. You are not doing an academic study in search of 'truth': your aim is to help move the group on in whatever way seems most achievable. Whatever route you take into a group will lead you eventually to the issues that need attention. The impact you can have will, however, depend on you and your style. This is more important than any specific methodology you use.

Phase 4 Feeding back the data

> *Critical question at this stage: How far does the client agree with your synthesis of the data?*

There is no point in collecting data for the event if you do not feed it back to the client in an actual discussion, not just an email exchange. At the feedback meeting you will need sensitivity that acknowledges the client's anxiety, defensiveness, fear and hopes. The ultimate aim is for the client group to own the results as part of the preparation for the time you will be spending together. Your data-gathering may contain some shocks for the client. Even where there is nothing that is actually new to them, they may reel from seeing and hearing it from a third party. During the meeting remember that client criticisms and defensiveness are not aimed at you personally. Use descriptive rather than evaluative words: be specific, brief, focused and crisp. Do not hedge the tough bits, do emphasize the positive and agree changes to any report you intend to present to the whole group.

Designing: basic principles

> *Critical questions at this stage: How can I design an event that meets the client's and group's needs and is also interesting, thought-provoking and lively?*

The overall aim of this phase is to consider the focus and purpose of the event you will be facilitating. Often it will need completely rethinking at this point, and a further discussion with the client will become an absolute necessity, as the experience of these facilitators makes clear:

> I interviewed the senior team individually. Far from seeing the main issue as the quality of customer care at the front end of the organisa-tion, they all saw it as a poisoned culture stemming from the Board and Executive team, of which my client was a member. After some blustering and protesting, all very understandable, my client agreed that we needed a total redesign of the day.

> A newly appointed boss wanted me to start the process of team-building. The interviews showed a preoccupation with one member: someone who everyone in the group believed had been the personal pet of the previous boss. This had been hinted at in my previous meeting with the boss but now it was on the table. We had to agree what, if anything, he was prepared to do, as to leave it to hang in the

air on the day was no longer possible and the nature of the event itself needed a radical re-think.

In designing an event, there are a number of factors it is useful to bear in mind.

How people learn: the learning cycle

The old Chinese saying put it best:

> I hear and I forget, I see and I remember, I do and I understand.

A facilitated day is built on this assumption – that we learn most readily when we actively participate. The idea of the learning cycle is also helpful. This was first advocated by the US academic David Kolb (1984) and his ideas have been widely accepted since. The assumption is that to learn, we need to experience a four-stage process (see Figure 3.2):

1 experiencing
2 reflecting and observing: thinking about the experience
3 theorizing: seeing where the experience fits in with theoretical ideas
4 applying and problem-solving: testing out the ideas and experiences and giving them a practical application

These ideas have been given further life by the work of Peter Honey and Alan Mumford (1992), who developed the idea that most of us do indeed learn best when learning encompasses the whole cycle, but that we also will tend to have one or two favoured styles. They developed a learning styles questionnaire to

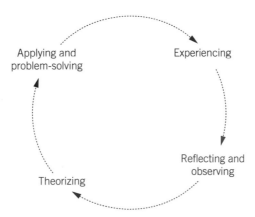

Figure 3.2 A four-stage learning cycle

identify which your favourite style or styles are. The categories reflect the Kolb learning cycle. You may be able to identify your own favourite through these descriptions (see Table 3.1).

Activists	
Like	**Dislike**
Doing and experiencing. Give them a role play or a game and they are into it before you have even finished giving them the instructions. Eager participants in discussion	Sitting around for too long; too much theorizing; anything that looks like slacking of the pace; working alone; reading
Reflectors	
Like	**Dislike**
Above all time – to think, to watch, to ponder. Want to see how others do things first. Enjoy reading. Need some solitude to absorb ideas	Being hurried; having to do things without preparation; going first; games and role plays where the intention is not crystal clear; crammed timetable; having to spend too much time with other people
Theorists	
Like	**Dislike**
Ideas and abstract concepts; knowing where something fits in with a general framework; being stretched by new notions; reading; lectures; analysis and logic	Ambiguity; open-endedness; anything that seems frivolous; not being able to question and be sceptical; timetables that lack structure
Pragmatists	
Like	**Dislike**
Activity that answers the question: what does this mean for me in 'the real world'?; opportunities to problem-solve; concrete application; useful tools and techniques	Anything that looks woolly or abstract; anything that seems set too far in the future to have meaning now

Table 3.1

These ideas are helpful. First, your own prejudices and inclinations will affect how you instinctively design the event. For instance, if, like me, your preference is to be 'activist', you will want to pack in far too much activity and will not allow for enough time to reflect. This will leave the 'reflectors' in your group highly frustrated. You may be drawn to theory – at the expense of the pragmatic – and so on. This, among many other reasons, is why it is an excellent idea to design an event with another facilitator as it guards against indulging your own prejudices and preferences.

Second, it is important to remember that all phases of the learning cycle need to be included. You can be flexible about this. You might think of the event as a series of mini learning cycles. For instance, you might have a 40-minute session in a facilitated event with a team where the activities listed in Table 3.2 happen.

This whole phase is relatively short, but each part of the learning cycle has been visited.

Varying the size of the group

Even where you are working with a small number of people, there will be advantages in varying the size of the group.

A group larger than six to eight people inhibits participation. In fact, participation diminishes sharply with the increase in the number of people. With six people, everyone will speak, even the most reticent. With eight people, two or three people will noticeably speak less. With 12, you will begin to see a

Activity	Comments
Team leader gives 10 minute highly structured introduction to possible changes coming up in near future, linking them to changes in the industry	Will appeal to the theorists
Facilitator invites 10 minutes of immediate discussion and reaction	The activists will spring to life
Each member of the group now spends five minutes solo encouraged to jot some ideas down on paper on the theme of 'how will this affect me?'	An activity for the reflectors
Whole group now discusses: what are the practical implications here for our business?	Will appeal to the pragmatists

Table 3.2

pattern where the most confident individuals speak a lot more than anyone else. By the time you get to more than 20, discussion may be dominated by two or three people. Varying group size also varies the tone, pace and style of the event and discourages too great a concentration of learning styles of one type. If you are able to influence the numbers attending the event, 12 is a magically useful number of people. You can work comfortably as a whole group, but the group can also split nicely into two sixes, three quartets, four trios or six pairs.

Where you use small groups, think carefully about any reporting back to the larger group. There is nothing more tedious than hearing four more or less identical presentations on the same topic. Avoid this by using some or all these tactics:

- Asking each group in turn for one idea from their group and then keeping on going around the groups in this way until you have exhausted their ideas.
- Giving each group a different brief.
- Strictly controlling the reporting back time to five minutes only.

Being realistic about time

In a whole-day facilitated event, you essentially have no more than six blocks of time available because you will be using at least 90 minutes for breaks of one kind or another. Never be tempted to try to stretch the time by lengthening the day or by asking people to go without breaks – the human brain and body simply do not cope well with this and the only result will be droopy or resentful people. I have a blank template in my computer with the typical slots shown in a grid. If you have the luxury of planning the day with a co-facilitator, then it can work well to draw out the same grid on a flip chart and to play with ideas by writing them individually on Post-it notes and shifting them around, adding some, removing others until you have a workable design.

Some design ideas

There is an inexhaustible store of ideas for use on facilitated events. My aim here is to give a flavour of some of those I come back to time and time again and is not intended to be a comprehensive collection. While some design ideas are multi-purpose, most fall into natural categories that match the flow of an event and that is how I shall deal with them here.

Warming up

Introduction from the leader/boss

The person who has commissioned you should start the event. Never let this morph into a full-scale speech or lecture where the boss drones on, killing the spirit of the occasion before it has started. Brief your client to spend five minutes and no more than ten minutes reiterating:

- The purpose of the event: something that combines challenge with optimism. It is important to have an upbeat tone.
- The specific outcomes he/she is looking for.
- The importance of everyone contributing their ideas freely.
- The role he/she will be playing during the day; that is, as just another participant.

When you have briefed yourself thoroughly, it is most unlikely that there will be any unpleasant surprises at this point. However, it is still possible. At one such event, despite having interviewed each member of his team, we had an explosion of emotion during the first half hour of an event I was facilitating for a directorate under extreme pressure after an unflattering report from its regulator. The moment the director, my client, had finished his five-minute intro, one of his colleagues suddenly dived underneath the table, pulled out a tottering in-tray, and shoving it forcefully across the table at his boss shouted, 'This is what I have to deal with! This is my in-tray and real work! If you think I've got time for this rubbishy event, then *you* deal with it!'

The group froze with horror, but my response was to say quietly that if he really felt he needed to return to the office to deal with this 'real work', then he should feel absolutely free to do so, and I waited calmly while he decided what he would do. Naturally, he stayed, though it did not surprise me to hear that several months later he had left the organization on what were described as health grounds.

Creating ground rules

Making a verbal contract with the group is an important way of building trust. It is also the way that you are explicitly granted the informal power to run the event. A contract is a two-way process: what you (group) expect from me and what I (facilitator) expect from you (group).

Some powerful questions here are:

- *How do you see my role?*

- *What can I most usefully do here?*
- (Where the group is going to meet over a period of time) *How should my role change as we get further into our meetings?*
- *What do you definitely not want me to do?*

This process surfaces the group's expectations and needs. Commonly, they will suggest that you challenge time-wasting, control the over-eloquent and offer feedback. It may also be useful to agree a set of ground rules around how the group wants to behave. These ground rules typically have two themes:

1. *Values-based behaviour*: A typical set of such ground rules might concern confidentiality, openness, trust and how the group wants to handle strong emotion.
2. *Practicalities*: mobiles, pagers, punctuality, whether or not it is all right to leave early, whether, if you are running the session on the group's premises, it is acceptable to return to offices during breaks.

Where groups are used to 'being facilitated' (or 'awaydayed to death' as one client described it wearily) this part of the discussion may be treated in a cynical, mechanistic way. If you think this is a risk, draw out from the group what behaviours will go with 'trust' and 'openness' by asking the following questions.

How would we know we were being 'open'?

What are the boundaries of the confidentiality?

Words like 'openness' and 'confidentiality' can trip far too easily off our tongues as participants and we may take them no more seriously than New Year resolutions – broken in the face of the first temptation. In fact, assume that they will be broken. Confidentiality in particular is easily agreed during the event, but it may be difficult to draw realistic boundaries for it in practice. You may also want to explore with the group how they want you to work with them on such issues. For instance, where strong emotion is concerned, you might want to say:

So if strong emotion appears in the discussion, how do you see my role here?

Keep the flip chart of ground rules visible so that when the group reviews its process, you – and they – can assess how far such ground rules were actually observed.

Your side of the ground rules process

The ground rules conversation is often conducted one-sidedly: a set of suggestions or demands from the group. In an adult–adult relationship the process of contracting should also model the partnership. Once you have heard the group's suggestions, to which you may or may not agree, it is appropriate to make your own, to which the group may or may not agree. These will depend on your own style and on the purpose of the event. My own suggestions all have to do with accelerating the process of creating trust.

Only one at a time: one problem, one person, one issue.

Suggesting this discipline to the group can have considerable impact on its ability to think creatively and to solve problems. What it means is helping the group to refrain from:

- interrupting
- drawing attention to their personal agenda
- giving advice
- telling irrelevant anecdotes (*in my department we . . .*)

Admitting to mistakes and uncertainties. If you do not understand or are puzzled, be prepared to say so. If you make a mistake, own up and apologize. If you are not getting what you want from the event, say so early and let us discuss it.

Say 'I' rather than 'one', 'people' or 'we'. This encourages everyone to own their opinions and to speak directly and personally. Model this practice yourself and encourage participants to do the same and to monitor each other. The exception here is that when the group arrives at the action phase, 'we' talk is correct because it represents collective will.

Taking risks. Be prepared to go beyond the normal protocols of your meetings.

Acknowledging feelings. It is all right to express feelings whether of anger, grief, joy, exhilaration, pleasure, sadness, disappointment. Feelings are part of the normal spectrum of human existence and acknowledging them is essential to robust problem-solving as well as to learning.

Ice-breakers

You have to start the event somehow, and ice-breakers will help. This is because when we come to an event, most of us still have at least half our minds elsewhere. We may be preoccupied with work or personal issues, we may be apprehensive about what will happen on the day itself, we may be wondering if the whole thing is going to waste our time. Icebreakers help because they give everyone (including you) the chance to become 'fully present'. They also help by obliging everyone to say something right at the start. The more the chance to speak is delayed, the less likely it is that the more reticent or less confident people will join in. Ice-breakers get people over the Inclusion phase of group development as speedily as possible.

These are the factors that will influence the type of ice-breaker you use:

- the subject and style of the event
- the participants and your best hunch about what they will like or dislike
- how well people already know each other
- the time available

Ideally, the best ice-breaker will be in keeping with the rest of the event. So if your event is to have a high level of personal disclosure, then you might want to risk having an intensely personal ice-breaker. If the event has a sober business focus then something more sober will be required. Inexperienced facilitators often overlook the simple mathematics of the size of the group and the time available. So if you have a group of 16 people and your ice-breaker requires each person to speak for two minutes, that will take 32 minutes of your timetable. This might be too much in a short event or it might be an excellent investment in a longer one.

Sample ice-breakers

Here are some ice-breakers that have worked for me:

- Ask people to write down on a scrap of paper the things that may distract them from the event. You then ask them to crumple it up and put it in a cardboard box that will be taped closed all day, promising them that they can retrieve their paper later if they wish.
  Comments: confronts the distraction issue head on. The physical process of writing it down and discarding it models the mental process. No one ever wants to retrieve their paper later: why would they? A variant is to ask people to state the same thing verbally.

- Ask people to put themselves into birth-order groups – only children, elder of two, eldest of three, youngest of three or more; younger of two, middle of three or more. The task is: what has your birth order contributed to (your management style/your attitude to being in a team . . .) or whatever the subject of your event is?

Comment: fun and surprisingly revealing. Gets people mixing in unexpected ways. Not so suitable for events where the focus is on business issues.

- Ask people to seat themselves in the order in which they joined the team/organization. The task: describe in no more than one minute what you noticed about this team/organization in your first week.
  Comment: an excellent ice-breaker for a day where one of the themes is change and how to manage it. People enjoy this one and it often says a lot about the organization. May take too long if you have a large group.

- Ask people to identify:
  - three things I want from this day are . . .
  - three things I can offer on this day . . .
  - my purpose in being here is . . .
  Comment: a reliable golden oldie. Not exciting, but works as a way of identifying what people want.

- Ask people to introduce themselves, name, job and what they would like to be doing if they were not doing their current job.
  Comment: the twist of asking for the third piece of information adds humour. People's fantasy jobs invariably fall into the following categories: rural escape (breeding puppies, living on an island); running a B&B or pub; travel; creative success (writing plays, novels, having an acting career) or splendid idleness.

- Ask people to find two other people in the room with whom they share a common interest. Encourage them to be creative and to go past the 'middle-aged man with two children' kind of response.
  Comment: only really suitable for groups of strangers; a good way of getting people to mingle at an early stage and produces a lot of good-humoured exchange. Like-minded people seem to have a nose for each other and this is a good way for them to meet sooner rather than later in the day. Negative: can seem contrived and mechanical.

- Tell people they will be swapping wallets. Give them the chance to remove anything that might be too personal or revealing. The task is to tell the rest of the group what they believe their partner's wallet says about them.
  Comment: highly revealing. If you doubt this, take a look now at your

own. A good way of conveying that you are working with the whole person and encouraging frankness. Negative: may be too personal for some people.

- Names ice-breaker: ask people to describe how they came by their name, either first or second name – or both. For example, how their parents came to choose their name, why they have changed, shortened, lengthened their first or second names.
  Comment: another highly revealing exercise that is essentially about identity and how we see ourselves. A surprising number of people have changed the names they were born with for a fascinating variety of reasons.

Analysing

This is typically part of the early stages of an event. There are many excellent tools for analysis to help people grapple with what may seem like a plethora of conflicting ideas. These approaches are among the classics.

SWOT analysis

Do not be afraid to use this classic just because many people will have done it before (see Figure 3.3). SWOT stands for: 'Strengths' – what are we good at? Weaknesses – what are we bad at? Opportunities – what is around the corner that could be a useful way for us to go? Threats – what could threaten our success? It can be applied to the total situation a group is in, or perhaps more usefully, some particular aspect of it; for instance, marketing, branding, competitive positioning and so on.

SWOT analysis can be done as a whole group or in small groups; for instance, with each of four groups looking at one quadrant.

PEST analysis

This is another reliable framework for analysing what the environmental pressures on a team or organization (see Figure 3.4). It is particularly valuable for groups that have become too inward-looking and are in danger of forgetting that the most intense pressure for change comes from outside not from inside an organization.

Stage 1   Ask the group to look at political pressures for change in their industry/organization as well as economic pressures, social and technological changes.

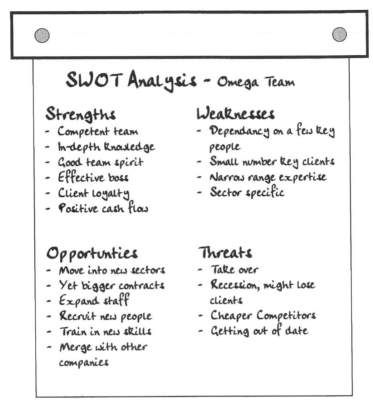

SWOT Analysis - Omega Team

Strengths
- Competent team
- In-depth knowledge
- Good team spirit
- Effective boss
- Client loyalty
- Positive cash flow

Weaknesses
- Dependancy on a few key people
- Small number key clients
- Narrow range expertise
- Sector specific

Opportunties
- Move into new sectors
- Yet bigger contracts
- Expand staff
- Recruit new people
- Train in new skills
- Merge with other companies

Threats
- Take over
- Recession, might lose clients
- Cheaper Competitors
- Getting out of date

Figure 3.3   Strengths and weaknesses analysis

What's going on in your world

Politically – locally and nationally?
What are the regulators doing or likely to do? Where are the pressure groups? Who or what are the most significant driving forces here?

Economically – what is the state of the local, national and international economy? Where are the driving forces here?

Environmentally – what is the global, national and local scene?

Socially – what is going on; for example, with the birth rate, ethnic and cultural composition, and age profile of the local/national population? What are consumers and users likely to want – what are they pressing for now?

Technologically – what are the technological drivers; for example, in pharmaceuticals, media, communications, transport, the Internet and other changes in computer technology?

Figure 3.4 Another popular analytical tool

What are driving forces inside the organization – what are the elements that are changing? What is likely to stay the same?

Stage 2 Ask the group to think about the implications of each of these for their work. Again, this can be done as a whole or small group activity.

Stakeholder analysis

This is an effective exercise for groups planning for change and who may have lost touch with meeting the needs of the people who one way or another pay for their existence. This is often true of professional groups used to self-regulation such as doctors or lawyers, or of providers of internal services to organizations.

Stage 1 Ask the group to identify its stakeholders – the people who can influence whether or not they get resources such as money, buildings, time, or decide whether or not the group may continue to exist. Normally, the stakeholders will be regulators, staff, clients/customers/users/senior management/ commissioners; media.

Stage 2   Now break the group into smaller groups and ask each to 'be' one stakeholder and imagine that it is two years from now. Your client group has been very successful. What has it done specifically that has pleased that stakeholder?

Stage 3   Bring the whole group together to hear a presentation from each stakeholder group.

Stage 4   Facilitate a discussion about what essential objectives come out of this for the group. NB it would be normal for there to be many conflicting objectives, but reconciling that kind of ambiguity is what organizational life is about.

Scenario planning

In thinking about strategic planning, most organizations assume a *'default scenario'* or a 'rear-view window' model that assumes the future is a continuation of the present and therefore predictable by studying current trends. Yet the default scenario is the one least likely to happen because sudden crises occur, combine with other unpredictable events thus producing shocks, surprises and discontinuities. Our responses are then dominated by panic and short-term thinking creating the quick fixes that merely generate further problems.

Scenarios are a way of organizing knowledge through stories. Scenario planning helps by looking ahead at uncertainties and untested assumptions. For instance, in the past people have confidently made these assumptions, all of which have proved wrong:

- The Cold War can never end.
- The US economy will always be strong.
- Home computers will never catch on.
- The Labour Party will never be electable.
- You cannot stop people smoking in pubs.
- Lack of democracy in China will always prevent its economy growing.

Scenarios are stories, not predictions. No one can predict the future. Unlike traditional business forecasting, they do not extrapolate trends from the present. They present plausible images of the future. The purpose of scenario planning is to help groups think hard about how prepared they are to face the shocks and crises of the future: how ready are we now if this future were actually to happen?

The stages are:

1 Identify the big questions: what are the real strategic challenges that face your team/organization? What are the big issues that will help decide your longer-term future?
2 Identify the driving forces using a PEST analysis.
3 What are the certainties?

In every scenario there are some certainties. For instance, you can predict the number of young adults there will be in any given population in 20 years' time by looking at the birth rate now; most governments in Western countries have a constitutionally limited lifespan.

Look here at:

- *slow-changing trends* – for instance, in infrastructure, populations, development of resources
- *constraints* – for example, regulator activity, legal obligations, media pressure
- *continuations* – major projects that are highly likely to continue; obligations that must be fulfilled, for example, IT commitments
- *clashes* – for instance, the growth of numbers of older people at the same time as there is a government refusing to provide extra benefits from raising taxes; continuing migration involving young families against the needs of the indigenous population

4 Identify the critical uncertainties.

This involves looking at cherished assumptions and also at worst nightmares. What could cause changes in any of the driving forces? For instance, could public opinion suddenly or slowly change on some topic of critical importance to your enterprise?

Some examples are:

- Could there be a further economic collapse of some kind? What might trigger that?
- Could there be an immediate environmental disaster?
- Could there be a serious pandemic?
- Could climate change suddenly accelerate?

- Could terrorist activity affect what we do?
- Could there be a significant shift in government policy affecting what we do?

5   Writing the scenarios.

Now develop three scenarios, a default scenario, an optimistic one and a pessimistic one using the factors you have identified. Write them as stories set five years ahead. Weave the elements together as a narrative and combining many of the uncertainties; for instance, an acceleration in climate change at the same time as immigration numbers increase dramatically along with a severe and prolonged recession. What would happen? Scenarios may be anything from 400 to 2,000 words. They are usually brief enough to be able to take in at a glance.

Finally, give your scenarios vivid and memorable names.

6   Discussing the scenarios: usually done in three separate groups who then present to each other. In looking at the scenarios:

- What light does it shed on the strategic issue you started with?
- How prepared are you to face this future now?
- Where would your strengths be?
- Where are your critical weaknesses?
- What should you do now to prepare for this possible future?
- How does this compare with what you are actually doing?

Appreciative Inquiry

Most problem-solving starts with what is going wrong – the word *problem* is itself the give-away. Paralleling the interest in positive psychology for individuals, there has also been a productive method of working on change by looking at what is going well in a group or organization rather than on what is going badly. The label 'Appreciative Inquiry' (AI) was coined in the 1980s by David Cooperrider of Case Western Reserve University (Cooperrider and Whitney, 2005). AI has become a 'movement' with enthusiastic disciples, a body of literature and its own training courses; in effect, a whole philosophy of change rather than just a 'technique'. This is just a brief summary of the overall approach and is not intended to be a substitute for in-depth reading and training.

The assumptions are:

- In any situation, however dire, there will be something that is going well.

- When this is analysed, this will have lessons for the future.
- Focusing on the positive creates energy for change.
- AI assumes that the group has its own answers – it does not need consultants to tell it what to do.

Enthusiasts for AI usually suggest that you approach it using the '5 D's':

1 *Defining*
The problem will be defined in a positive way – the language is important. So rather than saying 'We need to address the culture of blaming and avoiding responsibility in this team', you would define a positive outcome such as 'Create a culture of reward and responsibility in this team'.

2 *Discovery*
What is working well? Where are the success stories? What is motivating people? What stories can you tell about these successes? What conditions are creating this success? What can we learn from them?

3 *Dream*
'Dreaming' is about envisaging the future, based on the analysis that has come from the 'discovery' phase. How would we ideally like things to be? How might it look if we could apply all the conditions of the positive lessons to whatever the larger problems are?

4 *Design*
This is the phase of working out the practicalities. To make the 'dream' real, what systems, processes, people, tools and skills do we need?

5 *Deliver*
The action-planning and implementation phase.
The following example is from an organization development consultant:

> I was brought in to work with a team of 20 people working on a multinational project in an Asian country. The project was floundering. Interviewing everyone in the team revealed that no one really believed the project had much chance of success. There was a high degree of misery and a long history of difficult relationships between local and European staff all blamed on cultural, religious and language problems. However, applying the AI approach worked a kind of miracle that I could hardly believe. When I asked what in all this doubt and failure was actually working well, there was indeed one aspect of the project that was going brilliantly. When we asked this

little group, all working in an outpost office, to tell their stories it was clear that they had engaged a totally different approach from everyone else, working in an essentially flat hierarchy, had talked through the cultural difficulties candidly and had taken a creative slant on the actual project work. We spent a morning just teasing out what these ingredients were. It was the lever to solving the much larger-scale problems of the project as a whole.

Six thinking hats

This idea comes from the work of Edward de Bono (1989). His thesis is that we in the Western world have become undifferentiated and undisciplined in our thinking. He suggests that discussions often disintegrate because we confuse facts with emotion and speculation with facts. We may also find it difficult to disentangle gloom about what might go wrong with creative ideas about how to solve problems. The name of the technique comes from the metaphor of 'putting on your thinking hat'. De Bono suggests six. They offer a creative framework for looking all around an issue:

1   *White hat thinking*: what are the objective and verifiable facts? What data is missing? What might we have been assuming to be fact but is not?
2   *Red hat thinking*: what's the emotion around this issue? What is our gut response? What are the negative and positive feelings it creates?
3   *Yellow hat thinking*: what is the most optimistic way of looking at it? What might be the best possible outcome?
4   *Black hat thinking*: what could go wrong? What are the risks? What is the worst that could happen? Where are the weak spots?
5   *Green hat thinking*: what are the most creative possibilities here? What madcap ideas might there be around it?
6   *Blue hat thinking*: thinking about thinking. How can we take a measured and judicious view of the thinking that all the other hats has generated?

This is a flexible, enjoyable technique. At one point in our firm we did actually have sets of six baseball caps in the different colours for use at events. Ways of using the thinking hats approach include:

- Placing labels for the different 'hats' on six separate tables, dividing the group into pairs or trios and rotating them around the tables. Instruction: think about whatever the issue or problem is while 'wearing' the appropriate hat; write your conclusions on a flip chart.

- Talking through the problem as a whole group, visiting each 'hat'.
- Dividing the group into six small groups and asking each group to 'wear' one of the hats and then report back to the whole group.

Here is a manager-owner running a city-centre business in the hospitality sector talking about the benefits of the thinking hats approach:

> My business was facing a recession-created crisis. The hotel was doing OK but the restaurant was suffering. There was a general feeling of despair and a lot of unhelpful rumour. We spent the whole morning using the thinking hats. Using the white hat we identified growth in the lunchtime trade but a bigger decline than we had realised in the evenings. We had also tracked trends in room occupancy, showing that weekends were increasingly being undersold. The red hat yielded a lot of fear about possible job losses and a tendency to blame the directors. Black hat thinking saw us imagining further decline or even bankruptcy and also suffering because part of the hotel badly needed refurbishment and there was no way we could afford that. The most interesting hats were yellow and green, especially green where we came up with some amazing ideas. The upshot was that we decided to promote weekend breaks, make a modest investment in gourmet evenings through an informal dining club and also to dramatically expand our lunchtime trade through a 'street food' stall, – this one a high volume, low cost operation. This has been very successful. The positive publicity it generated raised morale and the whole thing was huge fun to do.

Five whys

This analytical tool works for problems that are not overcomplex. You start with the presenting problem and work backwards, asking a further 'why?' each time. Here is an example, used by a group of doctors:

- *Why are we getting too few patients reporting for cervical smear tests after we contact them?* Because they dislike the process.
- *Why do they dislike the process?* Because it is uncomfortable and embarrassing.
- *Why do they feel it is uncomfortable and embarrassing?* Because it is actually uncomfortable and because they can't guarantee seeing a woman doctor.
- *Why can't they guarantee seeing a woman doctor?* Because our appointment process is too rigid.

- *Why is it too rigid?* Because we don't make it clear in our letters that patients can request this and because we haven't briefed our receptionists.

This group of doctors actually answered the first question with a number of other suggestions, including: 'Don't feel they are at risk', 'Don't like the word cancer', and so on. They tracked back each of these suggestions using the same technique. The result was a rapid level of agreement about a new range of tactics that significantly increased the numbers of patients attending for the tests.

The Myers–Briggs approach to problem-solving

This is a reliable protocol based on the thinking behind the Myers–Briggs Type Indicator™ (MBTI) that sorts people into 16 personality types each with its different strengths and blind spots. The MBTI suggests that all of us have preferred 'mental functions' that are pairs of opposites. To take in information, you can be either 'Sensing', liking the practical, facts, detail and data of the here and now or Intuitive, liking what is intangible, possible, unique and focused on the future. To come to conclusions, you will have a preference either for 'Thinking', that is being objective, cool and rational or 'Feeling', where the emphasis is on relationships and human values. You do not need to be a trained MBTI practitioner yourself, or to have introduced the instrument to the group, to find it helpful.[1] The MBTI suggests that most of us can overuse our preferred style and underuse its opposite. This can lead to lopsided problem-solving. In most groups you will have a mixture of all four preferences. This exercise ensures that a more rounded approach to problem-solving is taken. The preferences are presented as a zigzag and suggests that in solving any problem you will need to ask:

- What are the facts? What are the data? This is the Myers–Briggs Sensing dimension – the realm of what you can see, hear, touch, taste and smell.
- What are the possibilities? If we had no restraints, what would be possible? This is the Myers–Briggs Intuitive dimension: what is intangible, around the corner, creative, in the future; what could happen?
- What are the logical implications of any choices we might make? This is the 'Thinking' dimension: the rational, analytical search for objective truth.
- What is the likely impact on people of any of our choices? This is the 'Feeling' dimension and concerns personal values and the human factors.

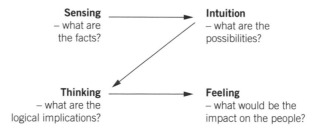

Figure 3.5   Using the Myers–Briggs Type Indicator for problem-solving

Improving relationships

Many events that need a facilitator are about getting the relationships on a more healthy footing. Again, there are hundreds of approaches here. All of them come down to finding ways for people to listen to each other. Here are just a few.

Perceptions exercise

This is a powerful activity and can provoke strong feelings; for instance, dismay, defensiveness, relief – the spectrum is wide. It works best where there is known difficulty between groups and also a willingness to begin the process of repair. The activity set out here is enough for a whole day's work. It cannot be rushed.

Divide the group into its natural constituent parts; for instance, PAs, senior managers; professionals, administrators; customers, suppliers.

Stage 1   Each group has the same task, to discuss:

- What do we think the other group (or groups) think about us?
- How do we see them?
- What would we ideally like them to think about us?
- What would we need to change in order to be seen by them in the way we would like?
- What would they need to do to improve the relationship between us?

Stage 2   Each group presents its results to the other groups. The other groups can ask questions for clarification – no more at this stage.

Stage 3   Each group resumes a discussion to discuss the other groups' perceptions of them. This may be combined with:

Stage 4   Each group decides what it can do at a practical level to meet what the other group or groups need.

Stage 5   Whole group agrees on action.

Prouds and sorries

This is a variant on the perceptions exercise. It can be done in a much shorter time.

Divide the group into constituent parts, as before. Give each group a single piece of flip chart paper. The task is to identify what they are most proud of as a group and what they are most sorry about; for example, where there have been collective failures or difficulties.

Now ask the group to treat each flip chart like a gallery and to pass slowly around the room reading them.

The final stage is to discuss the implications for each group in turn and then for the whole group.

Figure 3.6

Feedback exercise

This variant is always done one to one. It works well when the group has been working together for some time but there are many intensely felt personal difficulties. As a facilitator you should emphasize that people make their own choices about how much risk to take in the level of feedback they give to each other. It is also helpful to precede this activity by some structured guidance on how to give and receive feedback.

Explain that everyone in the group is going to give feedback one to one to everyone else in the group.

The time available is strictly limited to four minutes per pair; two minutes each. This is in order to encourage people to get to the point quickly. Apply this time limit strictly.

The format is:

- What I particularly appreciate about you is . . .
- What you might consider doing differently is . . .
- Things would be better between us if . . .

'Fishbowls'

Variants on these activities are also possible by using the fishbowl technique. What happens here is that one group sits in an inner circle and discusses a crucial topic, usually involving their perceptions of the other group. In the outer circle, the role is to listen carefully. As facilitator you will facilitate the inner group's discussion. The whole group then re-forms and the people who were in the outer circle get the chance to ask questions for clarification. The groups now swap over, with those who were in the outer circle taking the inner seats. The same process happens again.

In the discussion that follows, your role is to facilitate the whole group's understanding of the general themes that have emerged – usually that the views held by each group of the other have a large element of genuine mis-understanding and fantasy. The discussion usually also reveals that there are many simple, practical things that can be done if there is real willingness to change on both sides.

Drawing and other non-verbal techniques

- Give group members a range of art materials that might include pens and paints. You might also consider scissors, paste and magazines to cut up and make into a collage. Reassure them that no artistic ability is required. The brief may be tasks such as to create:

- a picture that represents both the inner and outer 'you'
- a heraldic 'shield' representing your life and values
- something that shows how you lead your life now and how you would prefer to lead it
- an image that represents how you see yourself in relation to the rest of the team, or how you see the whole team

Example (from a colleague):

> I gave everyone a plain brown paper bag of the type used in sandwich bars. There was a pile of glossy mags, some scissors and paste for everyone. Each person decorated the outside of the bag to represent the person they thought the world saw, then a piece of folded paper to go inside, also decorated, this time to represent the more private person. They took it in turns to present this to the group. It was interesting and very moving to listen to what people said. That team has never forgotten the exercise – it created higher levels of honesty and trust than they had ever achieved before.

- 'Statues'
  This exercise is sometimes called a group sculpt. Each person in turn silently arranges themselves and other people into a living tableau that represents how they see the group; for instance, how close or distant they feel they are from others in the group. Then, with facilitator encouragement, they rearrange the group as they would like it to be, followed by a whole-group discussion.

The well-functioning team

This is an effective activity for an intact team, or a group that needs to work together during the life of a project.

Stage 1   Give the group a set or sets of postcards on which you have written the characteristics of an effective team, one characteristic per card. Aim for between 20 and 30. These could be items such as: effective leadership, openness; effective communication when together; effective communication when apart; honesty; clarity of purpose; friendliness; conflict dealt with effectively; high standards of work; honest, frequent feedback; performance problems dealt with; good communication with other teams; autonomy; effective delegation; praise for work well done; stretching goals; clarity about roles; pride in the team; celebrating success – you can add any of your own personal beliefs about what will make a team work. Now ask the group to choose what they believe to be the most important 10 characteristics.

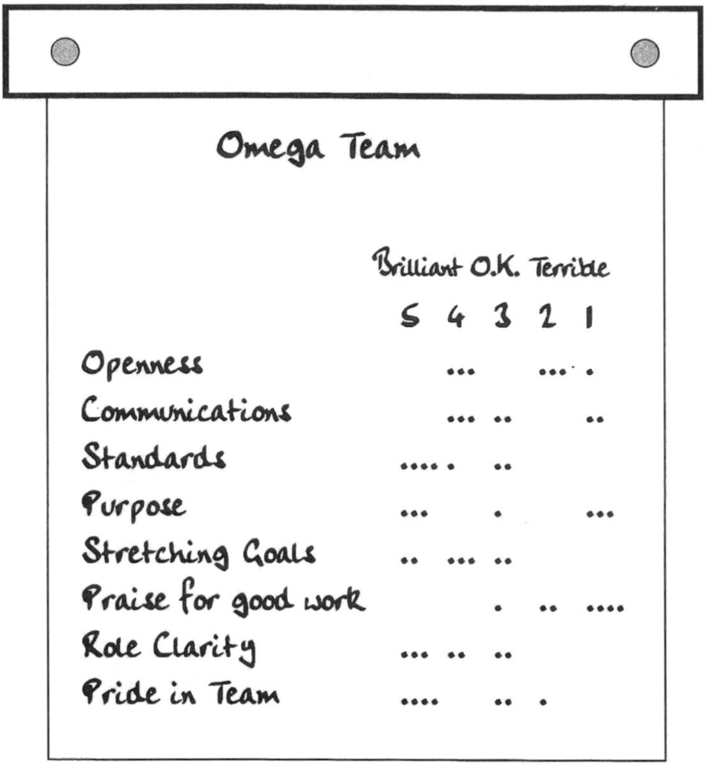

Omega Team

	Brilliant	O.K.	Terrible
	5 4	3	2 1
Openness		•••	•••·•
Communications		••• ••	••
Standards	••••• •	••	
Purpose		•••	• •••
Stretching Goals	••	••• ••	
Praise for good work		•	•• ••••
Role Clarity		••• •• ••	
Pride in Team		••••	•• •

Figure 3.7

Stage 2   Write the chosen characteristics on the flip chart with a 1–5 rating scale and ask the team to rate itself for current effectiveness. Give everyone 10 self-adhesive dots. This gives an immediate visual response – instant democracy.

Stage 3   Facilitate a discussion about how the group can move from where it currently is to where it wants to be.

If you are licensed to use the MBTI™, FIRO-B™ or other psychometric instruments, these are also wonderfully safe ways for the group to look at its relationships. The training for these instruments normally includes advice on how to use them with groups.

Creativity exercises

Brainstorming

This works well when the group has got stuck, new ideas are needed or there is low energy in the room.

Stage 1   The generation of ideas according to the rules below.

Essentially, you prohibit evaluation so what happens is that new, funny, inspirational, off-the-wall ideas are created, one building on the other. The process should be fast and furious. If it is a small group, get people to stand up and cluster around the flip chart. Explain that:

- everything anyone says is written down on a flip chart with no editing whatsoever
- everyone contributes their ideas
- any idea however preposterous is allowed, indeed encouraged
- no evaluation whatsoever is permitted at this phase – this includes funny looks, raised eyebrows and gestures as well as verbal responses

Stage 2   Highlight the most interesting ideas using a different coloured pen.
Stage 3   Agree the criteria for evaluating the ideas.
Stage 4   Evaluate the ideas against the criteria; for example, by starring some of them.
Stage 5   Agree how to take the ideas forward.

'Strawman' discussions

A 'Strawman' is an obviously wrongheaded, ill-thought-through and incomplete idea. Its aim is to stimulate creative discussion. This is how it works. The group agrees that it is facing a problem. Common ones would be: declining revenue; an eroded customer base; narrowed profit margins; restless or unhappy staff; and predatory competitors. Groups are formed where they briefly invent 'solutions' to the problem. These might be ideas such as:

- give away a substantial number of our services
- enter an entirely new market
- create a virtual office and sell the real one
- turn all staff into freelance associates
- reduce prices by 50 per cent

- appoint staff to the Board; negotiate a management buy-out
- make a significant capital investment of some kind

Each idea has a sponsor who makes as good a job as possible of presenting it. The idea is then critiqued with the aim of reducing the strawman to nothing. In doing so, a surprising number of genuinely new and useful ideas will normally emerge because the discussion enables rock-bottom assumptions to be identified and challenged.

Games

A 'game' is a puzzle of some kind that has to be solved by the whole group. Games are a way of increasing the energy in the group – the activists love them – but mostly they offer a metaphor for individual and group behaviour. A game may reveal with startling ruthlessness and brevity how a team or group usually behaves, especially when it is trying to solve problems. Most games work by depriving the group of some essential piece of information and by providing an ambiguous and difficult problem to be solved within a time limit. Games work because they offer a low-risk way for the group to see itself – a kind of mirror for how they are. The insights are usually powerful. For instance, I introduced a team I was working with to the game Blindfold Square. The game is simple. All it needs is a blindfold for each person in the group and a long length of rope or clothes line. The group puts on the blindfolds and you tell them that their task is to make a perfect square, held at waist height, out of the rope. The combination of the silliness of the task and the deprivation of all the usual visual clues is what make this a revealing game. In this case, the game showed the following to the group:

- It over-relied on its boss – no one else in the group was able to take a lead.
- Some people stood on the sidelines far too soon and became spectators.
- The most junior people in the team were not listened to, even though they were the ones who came up with the best ideas about solutions.
- The team was sloppy about its quality standards.

This was what happened in the game, but it was also, they all agreed, exactly what happened in real life too.

Another well-known game is Red-Black, also known by a number of other colour names such as Blue-Red. The game is intended to explore issues of values, trust and negotiating style.

The group divides into two and goes to separate rooms. There are 10 rounds.

The facilitator tells the groups that the only purpose is to end the game with a positive score and explains the scoring system (see Table 3.3).

The facilitator travels between rooms, telling each group how the other has voted and scored and keeping a tally of scores. There is an opportunity to negotiate new rules between rounds 6 and 7 and rounds 9 and 10, when each team nominates and briefs a person to represent them in a discussion run by the facilitator. Although it is obvious that everyone can win simply by 'playing' black every time, the temptation to dish the other group is usually overwhelming. In the debrief that follows, some helpful questions are:

- How do people feel now this minute?
- What happened to principle?
- How were minority views handled in the groups?
- How far does this represent the way influencing and negotiating are normally handled both by individuals and by the whole group?
- How realistic is it to suppose that there can always be a win-win outcome?

Making games safe and effective

Games are emotionally arousing: do not introduce them if you feel you might be unable to handle what could follow. Participation should be voluntary – if people do not want to take part, let them be observers or absent themselves altogether if they prefer. Always explain the rationale behind introducing a game and devote ample time to the debrief where you ask about links from the game to the everyday life of the group. Take care with the physical and psychological aspects of safety; for instance, if someone tells you that they would feel claustrophobic wearing a blindfold, just accept it. If you are working out of doors, assess the site for safety risks.

There are hundreds of possible games, all with their unique advantages

If the teams play		They will earn these scores	
Team A	Team B	Team A	Team B
Black	Black	+3	+3
Red	Black	+5	–5
Black	Red	–5	+5
Red	Red	–5	–5

Table 3.3 The scoring system for the Red–Black game

and disadvantages. Search the Internet for sites devoted to this topic, or even better, consult other facilitators about games they have found effective.

Decision-making techniques

The normal rhythm of a facilitated event is to start with the warm-up, then proceed to analyse whatever the problems are, then to use creativity techniques to expand people's minds and loosen their attachments to old mindsets and then to narrow down the possibilities through decision-making.

Innumerable problems can arise at this point in the event, such as:

- The group believes it has the power to make a decision when in fact it does not; it is merely being asked to recommend.
- There is no discussion about what processes to use to make the decision.
- The discussion becomes polarized and tetchy.
- Groupthink (see Chapter 2, p. 38) takes over and no one voices their disagreement even if in fact everyone disagrees, so everyone agrees to what no one privately believes is the right thing to do.
- Inappropriate decision-making techniques are employed.

Voting

The oldest decision-making technique in the world is the vote. It is quick and it is apparently decisive. Why, then, is this such a bad idea for a facilitated event? Voting is divisive. The defeated group may feel bitter; the vote does nothing to help them live with the option that has won more votes so it may perpetuate the very divisions it has been designed to prevent. Voting encourages black and white thinking and also a premature close to discussing options, whereas shades of grey may be more useful and lead to more productive thinking. Finally, depending on what type of voting method is used, it can create pressure to conform; for instance, if a show of hands is used. If your group insists on voting, you can soften the worst aspects by trying any of these tactics:

- asking the opponents of each option to summarize the view with which they disagree. This forces attention on the positives in the opposite view
- setting up a pair exercise where you do the same as above
- introducing a matched time period for each side to put their views
- changing the usual 50 : 50 ratio to something different; for example, 60 : 40
- suggesting a recess while people consider their views

Discussing the process of decision-making

Groups can quickly get into emotionally heated discussions about a decision. One of the main reasons this happens is that they have neglected to discuss how a decision is going to be made. Instead, the focus is on what the decision should be. People endorse one view and then back themselves into the corner of defending it at all costs. You can pre-empt this by insisting on a discussion of how the decision might be made, offering a number of alternatives, such as those that follow here.

Multi-voting

This is a technique with many applications. Essentially, you are asking people to spread their preferences among several options. It is more democratic than straight voting and enables people to feel that at least their preferences have had an airing.

Creating criteria

This simple tool is significantly underused. Where you can see that a group is likely to have trouble with a decision, ask them to agree criteria for making the decision first. Ask:

What would the features of a good decision be?

The answers may emerge readily, or they may again be the focus of disagreement. In this case, consider using a decision grid that allows weighting of the criteria. Table 3.4 shows one such list generated by an architectural practice that was considering what kind of building they needed for new offices. The discussion had generated a high level of emotion and it was clear that there were widely differing assumptions.

   The facilitator then handed everyone four sticky dots, enforcing the rule that you could only vote once (i.e. one dot) for your favourites. This clearly revealed that there were four important criteria on which everyone could agree: cost, central location, an aesthetically pleasing building and a good fit with the company's brand. Happy smiles all round.

   The same technique can be used in a forced-choice protocol to decide between confusing or divisive options against the criteria. In this case the question is:

How well in your view do these options stack up against the criteria?

Give everyone a limited range of votes/dots (four in the example here shown

Criterion	Votes – one dot each per item!
Cost-neutral	
Five-year lease, renewable	
Centrally located: easy access to at least three tube lines	
Disabled access	
Purpose-built block	
Natural light everywhere	
South facing	
Eco-friendly/obviously a 'green' building	
Aesthetically pleasing	
Doesn't look lavish/over the top	
Good fit with our brand: excellent 'calling card' for us	
Enough space for visiting associates	
Potential for remodelling: putting our unique stamp on it	
Space for bike park outside	

Table 3.4

in Table 3.5) again reinforcing the only-one-vote-per-item rule to stop people using all their votes for a favourite option.

Options	Cost	Central location	Aesthetics	Fit with brand
Keppoch St				
Exmouth House				
St John's Building				

Table 3.5

To minimize any problems with using multi-voting, ask group members to vote by filing individually behind the reversed flip chart so that they have privacy, or use Post-it notes as ballot sheets that are handed to you. This prevents people being over-influenced by others and preserves anonymity. Sometimes multi-voting does not yield a clear result, in which case you might want to narrow the options and repeat the process or else give differing weightings to the dots/votes.

The line-out

Where a group is divided on a decision, there will be a temptation to force closure by suggesting a vote or some other exercise that brings the discussion to what could be a premature end. If you suspect that this might happen, you could try the following:

- Ask one person in the group to pose the question as clearly as possible, setting out the two choices.
- Get the group to stand up. Tell them that there is now an imaginary line from one side of the room to the other. Each end of the line represents one of the two possible choices.
- Ask people to place themselves along the line according to where their own opinion falls. When they have done this, ask each person to say briefly why they have placed themselves where they have.

This exercise usually reveals a wide range of opinions with many people clustered in the middle and will normally bring a depth that could have been lacking in the previous discussion.

Force field analysis

Force field analysis is many decades old but none the worse for that. It was developed by Kurt Lewin (p. 28) the early exponent of organizational development and action research in psychology. The idea is that in any proposed change, the human ability to drag our feet will be visible and should be anticipated. There will be forces pushing for change and forces pushing against – the forces of resistance. The chances of any proposed change taking root are increased when the forces in favour are more powerful than the forces of resistance (see Figure 3.8).

How to use the tool
This structure is helpful:

1   Describe the present state.
2   Describe the ideal solution.
3   What will happen if you do nothing?
4   List all the forces driving change towards the ideal outcome.
5   List all the forces of resistance.
6   How valid are each of these forces? Which are the most important?
7   Give a score to each of the forces using a numerical scale; for example,
     1 = extremely weak and 4 = extremely strong.
8   Write them in on the chart, representing each according to its
     strength.

Once you have got the group to identify the items on each side, the discussion
is then:

> *What needs to happen to increase the forces for change?*
>
> *What needs to happen to reduce the forces of resistance?*
>
> *How might we inadvertently create new resistance if we strengthen the change forces?*
>
> *If we did, how would we counter them?*

Assessing buy-in

Sometimes it can happen that there is a false consensus. People withhold their
objections, only naming them at the very last moment, or worse, when the

Change forces				Ideal solution	Resistance forces			
Strength					Strength			
1	2	3	4		4	3	2	1

Figure 3.8   Force-field analysis

event is over. This can matter hugely when the stakes are high and the apparently consensual decision is undermined later by rumour and backbiting.

To prevent this happening, test the buy-in to important decisions. Ask the group to vote anonymously on how far they personally endorse an important decision, giving their views a percentage (see Figure 3.9). Represent the result so that everyone can see it.

This may reveal that no one gives above 70 per cent to the decision, in which case it may be the wrong decision and the group might want to reconsider its verdict. There may be a wide range of votes – also a sign of trouble. Alternatively, there may be just one or two people who have given low percentages. If so, invite them to identify themselves. When they do, ask them what would need to happen to raise their levels of personal commitment. This will usually result in a productive discussion, often one that changes some relatively small part of the total package but greatly increases the chances of the decision having a positive impact because everyone endorses it.

The action phase

Remember that any facilitated event is about change. To have any impact on the issues identified by the group, the event will need to end with an action plan. There are a number of familiar traps here:

- The action phase is rushed – people are already beginning to shuffle with their belongings ready to leave.
- The conscientious people volunteer for most of the tasks; everyone else is strangely silent.
- Leaders of teams get landed with much of it because they care most.
- There are far too many items on the list.
- The tasks are vague, enormous or both.
- There are no penalties for lack of follow-through.

Preparation is once more the main way to forestall any of these pitfalls. As part of your preparation, ask straightforwardly what the group's track record is of following through. Where there have clearly been problems, investigate the root causes. This is what one of my colleagues found when he asked these questions:

> In doing my pre-event interviews, I discovered that there was widespread cynicism about whether anything would change, or indeed whether it was possible for anything to change. The general view was that they were suffering from 'initiative overload', that all previous awaydays had ended with long 'to-do' lists, none of which had ever actually been done. The whole team was in a state of inertia.

What percentage buy-in do you privately give to this decision?

10	20	30	40	50	60	70	80	90	100

Figure 3.9 Percentage buy-in to decisions

To get around these problems, take a few moments to remind people of these traps. Ask the group for their own ideas on getting around them. Normally, people will suggest making a variety of sensible strategies. For instance, restricting the list of actions to no more than some small number; spreading the load between the group; devising a method of accountability; making the actions specific and measurable; and suggesting short-, medium- and long-term actions.

A familiar grid will normally help this process (see Figure 3.10). Your role in the discussion is to challenge any tendency to overload individuals, to insist on specifics and measurables, to raise the whole question of how progress will be tracked and to ask the question, *'What might sabotage these action plans?'* Then depending on the answer, *'What needs to happen to ensure that there really is follow-through?'*

Ask who is going to type up and distribute the notes from the day. The quicker these are sent out, the more likely it is that the action plan will actually be implemented.

Large group interventions

The most familiar form of facilitated event is the small group that is planning for some kind of organizational transformation in a traditionally top-down

Action	Whose responsibility	By when
1		
2		
3		
4		
5		
6		

Figure 3.10 Action planning

process. Typically, this will be the executive team. But there is another whole genre of events, usually known collectively as *large-group interventions*. Like so much else in working with groups, the philosophy and practicalities originated with the Tavistock Institute (p. 29). In 1959 Eric Trist and Fred Emery, two Tavistock consultants, ran a five-day conference in Bristol with the newly created Armstrong Siddeley company. It was based on the principle that the group itself would know what was best for its future if it worked on establishing a vision of how it wanted to be and then worked on how to close the gap between this desirable future and the present. The number in the group was small. However, the thinking behind it, and the way that thinking was translated into a workable methodology, was the forerunner of all the types of large group events from which we can choose today.

Devotees of large group interventions point to the many reasons that conventional approaches to change do not work: for instance, how they perpetuate the fantasy that leaders can control all the deciding and problem-solving, or that change can and should be based on the cascade principle. This is why conventional staff conferences will tend to have such a stiff, over-produced feel where information is meticulously combed of anything that could seem risky, taboo areas are carefully skirted and participation is kept to a respectful minimum. The whole event reinforces the idea that there are authority figures who know best and that change can be planned.

Large group interventions are based instead on 'systems thinking' – the idea that 'the system' is broader than just the organization or the immediate team: it will include clients and customers, competitors, regulators, partner organizations and other social networks. Change is assumed to be messy and complex with no easily discernible causes and effects. When you do not take the system into account you may make lopsided and short-range decisions. Large group interventions aim to tackle all these shortcomings by working instead from these principles:

- Change works best when you involve all the stakeholders even if there are areas of violent disagreement among them.
- Long-term change is more likely when the people who will have to implement it are also involved in diagnosing what the problems actually are.
- Even if it is difficult, cooperation works better than domination.
- Going with the flow is better than wasting energy on the futile task of trying to be in control at all times.
- It is more productive to create optimism by working on possibilities and then working backwards to the present than to work 'cold' on solving problems.
- People want to take responsibility for anything that affects them.

Involvement produces superior ideas and is more likely to produce change that sticks.

At the event itself, the principles are also the opposite of the overgroomed, tightly managed traditional conference. At a typical large group intervention the assumptions are that all perceptions are valid and all participants equal. Numbers of participants may be anything from 10 to 2,000. Open, frank dialogue is the core of the event. People come as volunteers not as representatives. You do not need ice-breakers, presentations or games. It takes an enlightened client to commission one of these events. Clients have to be prepared to acknowledge a counter-intuitive truth that where they do not know 'the answer', it is better to let it emerge from listening to others. Indeed, in my own experience, selling the idea of this kind of event to a client who is understandably freaked by the apparent risks is harder than anything you will need to do on the day. These approaches have been widely used in communities where there are large numbers of people who would be regarded as marginalized; for instance, an aboriginal group in Australia working to improve access to education by their own people. Equally, they have been successful in hard-edged commercial environments such as Ikea where junior staff have generated many commercially successful ideas.

Types of large group event

Many different types of large group event have emerged in the last 30 years, all closely related to each other.

Future search

This normally involves 60+ people with the aim of replicating 'the system' and then 'bringing it into the room' for the purpose of strategic planning. It was developed by Marvin Weisbord (Weisbord, 2004; Weisbord and Janoff, 2000). Usually, this is a two-day event with five phases:

1   reviewing the past as a giant timeline where personal, community and organizational events are tracked and charted
2   mapping the present where people sit in their professional or interest groups (typically eight people sitting at round tables) and examine their relationships with the question/organization commissioning the conference
3   creating the ideal scenario, often presented as a skit, this time working in so-called max–mix groups
4   identifying the common ground and creating a shared vision
5   drafting plans to implement the changes that will make the vision real

Pluses: this is a highly structured framework inside which a great deal of variation is possible. It is ideally suited to any project that needs major impetus at its start; for instance, an organizational merger. Drawing on multiple perspectives and mixing people constantly from different parts of the system means that barriers are dismantled and common ground is identified.

Minuses: the hard work is in the planning. It needs a dedicated project group that can give it enormous amounts of time. As a facilitator, this is where you will add value. As with all such large-scale events, logistics are complex; for instance, group membership is constantly rotated during the day according to a pre-agreed plan and this needs to be carefully considered in advance and then clearly signposted on the day. Staff time and the time commitment of those attending can also be a deterrent so it needs a zealous and influential in-house sponsor; ideally, someone who has already seen the benefits as a participant elsewhere.

The Conference Model

The purpose of the Conference Model is to fast-track the redesign of an organization. Usually, the need for this will have been made apparent by some kind of crisis. Like Future Search, it usually involves between 60 and 80 people for each event, but unlike Future Search, there are four consecutive events, each lasting two days:

1 The visioning conference: this resembles a future search event.
2 The customer/supplier conference where the focus is on how customers and suppliers currently see the organization and how they would like it to be in the future.
3 The technical conference where business processes are tracked with a view to simplifying them and improving quality.
4 The organizational design conference that gathers feedback from the other three events and decides on the new design of the organization.

There are many other variants of these events, including Real Time Strategic Change and Simu-Real.

Open Space

This is my personal favourite. Compared to other large group techniques it needs no elaborate planning. I find Open Space exhilarating – and terrifying. Every time I run one I wonder if this will be the time the model doesn't work – but so far it always has. Open Space was invented by Harrison Owen (1997) in the 1980s when it struck him that people constantly described the coffee breaks and mealtimes as the most productive parts of any meeting. Why not, then, turn the whole event into something informal that tackles all the subjects that people really want to talk about? It is a method that is designed to solve complex problems in the shortest possible time and can work with as few as 10 people or as many as several hundred. It may last half a day or as long as three days.

What happens in an Open Space

The organization has a perplexing problem, possibly one that is full of conflict and which has defeated everyone. The problem is posed as a set of questions. Typically, this would be: What is the future of X? (the issue). What do we need to do to resolve it? An invitation is sent out to everyone who might care about finding the answers, but attendance is voluntary and no one comes as a 'representative'. The group sits in an open circle or two concentric circles. The facilitator stands in the middle and introduces the 'rules'. These are:

- *Whoever comes is the right people.*
- *Whatever happens are the only things that could happen.*
- *The law of two feet* means that if you are not getting what you want, move on to somewhere else.
- *Butterflies and bumblebees are fine:* butterflies are people who stand around looking beautiful and may attract others to come and join them. Bumblebees go from group to group bringing ideas with them as they go.
- *When it's over, it's over.*

The facilitator describes what will happen during the rest of the day, then reminds people of the question/problem and invites anyone who has an idea that they feel is related to finding the answer to the problem to come forward, say their name, briefly name the topic and write it on a piece of paper. At first only the most confident come forward but through encouragement, patience and perhaps a little coaxing, eventually many dozens of possible topics are identified. This process may take up to 40 minutes. There is a large blank timetable running along one wall and 'The Marketplace' follows. This is where the people who have nominated topics choose a room and stick their piece of paper to the blank space on the timetable. Many topics will be similar so some negotiation takes place at this point. People then take themselves to the rooms and topics that interest them, roaming from room to room if they wish. The groups facilitate themselves and produce a flip chart sheet of recommendations. These in turn are attached to another wall. In a one-day Open Space, about three-quarters of the way through the event, the whole group will reconvene. As facilitator you and your client will have met at some point and identified the main themes. You may then go through the whole process again or it may be obvious which the action points are. Project teams are then assembled around these themes – again on a volunteer basis – and discuss next steps. The event ends with a 'closing ceremony' where anyone who wishes to speak can walk into the reassembled circle to pick up the 'talking stick' (a microphone if it is a large group). All the flip charts are typed up and swiftly distributed to everyone who attended, together with progress reports from the action groups.

Advantages and disadvantages of Open Space

The beauty of the Open Space approach is that there is no place for cynicism or acting out. There is a buzz of optimism and energy. If as a participant you have a topic that you feel is vitally important, then you will have your chance to raise it and if you do not take that chance then you have to live with the consequences. You cannot moan that 'no one ever pays attention to the real issues'. Senior people in the organization can get some salutary shocks. In one organization where I ran an Open Space, the executive team discovered that far from being the heroes to their people that they had imagined, they were widely held in disrespect – and they found out why, then what to do about it. In another company, complacency about customer service was well and truly banished as the most junior staff enthusiastically redesigned the delivery process, resulting in a 100 per cent increase in profit the following year. One of the most moving Open Space events I have ever facilitated was for a British organization operating in a country that had formerly been part of the Soviet bloc. The question for the event was: *What do we need to do to guarantee a successful future for this operation?* The event ran in four languages: English, Russian, the language of the country and German. It involved every single person on the staff from the most senior managers to the cooks and drivers. On the second day, several staff approached me shyly to ask whether it was really true that they could choose which groups they went to, and really true that they could wander from group to group. As one of them said, 'You've got to remember that memories of the Soviet era die hard and democracy is still very young here'. In two days this organization had created, or possibly recreated, commitment to its overarching purpose, had sketched out a viable business plan, had involved all staff in what it should contain, had planned improvements to its services, had agreed training plans for everyone and had also enjoyed itself hugely.

The disadvantages of Open Space are that it cannot work when senior managers secretly believe they already have the answer to the question. When you describe it to clients, it can sound flaky: 'Hippy heaven' as one of my clients snorted in response to my first attempt at persuading her to undertake it. They may feel uneasy about the apparent lack of structure, or tell you than 'no one' will come forward with ideas (I have never known this happen). In fact, there is an underpinning structure, but it is a *process* and not a *content* structure and this can unnerve people who like to feel in control. As a facilitator you have to be able to hold on to your courage at the point where the 'Marketplace' starts. It can seem chaotic and noisy, but trust the process: it works, and miraculously people quickly go off to their chosen sessions. Follow-up to the event is important, but this is no different from the care you need to take at any other facilitated event to ensure that the energy and impetus of the day is not lost in good intentions that never result in change.

Large group logistics

These are powerful approaches to problem-solving. However, they create logistical demands. If this is not your forte, you will need to work with someone specializing in these troublesome practicalities. You need at least one very large room – hotel ballrooms or public assembly rooms are ideal. You will need one well-equipped breakout space for every 10 people and enough wall space for substantial numbers of flip charts. With a large group you will need many sets of flip charts, dozens of pens and also microphones. It helps to have several laptops available so that the output of sessions can be keyed in immediately and then emailed to every participant.

There is only space for an introduction to these methods here. For a comprehensive account of the various large group interventions and how to run them, consult the excellent book by Barbara Bunker and Billie Alban (1996). Even better, beg or blag your way into another facilitator's session in order to see at first hand how powerful the methodology is.

Note

1   My own book on the MBTI (2007b) gives more information on the 16 personality types.

4　The room and other practicalities

Room service? Send up a larger room.

(Groucho Marx, comedian and actor)

The practicalities matter.

Start with what you are setting out to achieve. Good questions here are:

- What is the purpose of the meeting? For instance, if it is to generate creative ideas then what kind of environment will encourage this? If it is to calm down highly stressed people, then a quiet pleasant venue will be essential.
- How many people will be there? What size room do you need?
- What kinds of activity are likely on the day? For instance, if you plan 'games' you may need extra space.
- How much small group work will there be? If the answer is 'a lot' then you will need enough well-equipped break-out rooms to accommodate discussion.
- What kind of discussion is likely when you split the group up into smaller groups? If it is intense pair work on highly personal topics, for instance, then noise from other pairs can be intrusive.
- Can the venue provide the equipment you need?
- How far can you rely on your liaison person at the venue to fulfil their promises?
- How flexible is the venue about meal times?

The more you can influence the choice of venue, the better the event is likely to be. Remember that the room has significance in its own right. Ideally, it should be neutral territory, not associated with any one person's status and trappings and even more ideally in a different building from any that the participants use every day. Being in their normal building can mean the likelihood of normal thinking prevailing and can also encourage people to drift off during the breaks to play with their emails.

Much facilitation unfortunately has to take place in appallingly unsuitable places:

> Got to the venue and found that the group was to meet in a room on the unheated top floor of a deserted office block. It was full of abandoned, battered furniture. Some other poor group had been meeting there the night before and their dirty cups were still there. I rang the facilities manager and was told that the lift did not serve this floor so it would take him a while to sort everything out. Since the group was meeting to discuss customer care, it had its ironic side.

> Wonderful hotel in the Cotswolds. Only trouble was, the whole workshop depended on being able to cover flip chart pages with writing and let everyone see them. The hotel had hand-blocked wallpaper and made a point of telling us that the last company that had stuck things on the walls had been pursued with a bill of several thousand pounds to replace the wallpaper.

Budget

Now that newspapers take such a keen interest in how organizations, especially those in the public sector, spend their money, the choice of venue has become tricky. We have all seen headlines with the apparently horrifying news that a government department team spent thousands of pounds on a two-day event, sneeringly referred to as 'a bonding session'. This is journalistic shorthand for 'rubbishy event where managers (implied: who needs 'em anyway?) indulged themselves at the taxpayers' expense'. Often when you look at the sum quoted, it is in fact eminently reasonable. Participants themselves may complain at the seeming luxury of the venue.

A friend works as an internal facilitator in a large hospital and I like the way she deals with such queries. These invariably come from suspicious senior doctors who may believe that spending on a conference centre means money snatched directly from the care of patients. My friend, who by the way chooses pleasant but modest local hotels as venues, politely asks the concerned doctor if special environmental conditions are needed for his own work. Eagerly falling straight into her trap he replies that it is – he needs a first-rate operating theatre, consulting room or laboratory. My friend sweetly replies that the same applies to her work. To do it well, she, too, needs a purpose-designed environment. A scruffy or obviously cheap venue is rarely a good idea:

> I could not believe that my client had chosen such a terrible place.

I honestly thought that Fawlty Towers hotels had disappeared but this one was a rabbit warren of horrible little rooms, badly equipped for conferences. The meeting room was dark and gloomy. Two people's cars were vandalised on our first night there and that just about summed it up. The awful venue cast despondency over the whole event.

In effect it was a student hostel. It might have been OK for school parties, which was how they did most of their business, but I did not appreciate the hard narrow beds or the sliced-white toast and tinned grapefruit for breakfast.

Clients may choose such places out of fear that anything more expensive could land them in the *Daily Mail*. However, this may be a short-term tactic that rebounds. When I have been obliged to run events at nastily cut-price conference centres, the participants invariably react with dismay. A wonderful place does not guarantee success, but a poor one really gets in the way. In general, we expect venues to be at least at the standard of our own homes. Anything less is immediately noticeable and you will struggle to overcome the negative atmosphere it creates.

Other considerations

If the event is residential then aim to ensure that everyone has identical rooms as far as possible. Senior people – and indeed facilitators – should have no privileges. If there are a favoured few who boast about their four-posters, special suites, bowls of fruit, upgrades and the like this will create gossipy speculation, unease – or actual fury – in those not so lucky.

Lighting

A room that has no natural light will create an impression of imprisonment and will become oppressive. Even with actual windows the view may not be pleasant: I have worked in rooms facing rubbish dumps, blank grey walls and dismal alleyways. The view will affect the mood in the room. Ideally, it should be pleasant but not distracting. At a recent conference I attended, there was natural light in one break-out room but the light was filtered through floor-to-ceiling opaque glass with a busy street on the other side. As the session went on, we in the audience became increasingly transfixed by what looked like giant shadow puppets on the window as the passersby in the street stopped for chats or rearranged their shopping. The style and amount of artificial lighting matters. Hotel rooms are often too dark, designed for romantic dinners, or wedding receptions, not for business discussions. The reverse can also be alarming. I remember an event in a purpose-designed training centre that had cruelly glaring strip lighting everywhere. The feeling of being in an interrogation centre was overwhelming, an impression increased by noticing that other events there seemed to be dominated by Customs and Excise staff. These appeared to be practising their anti-smuggling handcuffing skills in the corridors (though I think I may have made that last bit up – it just felt like it in retrospect).

Noise

I stopped booking one nicely equipped London conference centre when I realized that most of the rooms faced a busy street market and that the windows were single-glazed. The local binmen trundled along several times a day together with perpetually slow-moving traffic and much horn-honking from frustrated drivers. At one venue on the English coast, I was facilitating a discussion with an executive team on their home territory when we were interrupted by an enormous seagull that interspersed loud screeches with rapping its beak imperiously on the window. 'Oh don't worry', said one of the participants airily, 'that's just George as we call him. Throw him one of those biscuits and he'll shut up.' Air-conditioning is noisy but it is usually there because the room gets too hot without it, so if you turn it off, you and your group will stifle. Natural ventilation is better but not if it means letting in noise and pollution.

Environment

The environment around the venue also has an influence. When people can go for a pleasant walk during breaks or do a little light window-shopping, it can make all the difference to the mood during the day. A usable outdoors also gives you more possibilities for activity during the event.

Seating

If the chairs are uncomfortable you and your group will be fidgety all day. Dainty gilt chairs that are fine for wedding receptions are not suitable for business meetings. Chairs should have some lumbar support, be generous enough to accommodate those with larger bottoms and be specially designed for conferencing. Hotels will often expect you to work in rooms with quirkily mismatched sofas and chairs. The agile people head for the squashy seating while others perch at different heights on hard upright chairs. When your aim is equality in participation and uncomplicated discussion, you are immediately at a disadvantage if the seating means that some people are lolling deep in a sofa, their feet hugging the floor while others have their legs dangling from over-high dining chairs. Ideally, all the chairs should be identical and comfortable enough to sit in all day.

Client service

You should expect minimally a dedicated conference manager, instant response to requests for help and flexibility about mealtimes. Personally, I do not appreciate venues that insist on a school-dinners' approach to lunch, where there are rigid 'sittings', invariably too early or too late.

Sometimes the impetus and magic of the occasion overcomes even the most unimpressive or peculiar venue. I still remember fondly an event in mid-Wales with a lively social services team. There was a sudden severe November snowstorm with accompanying prolonged power cut in the middle of our first day. We were at a simple B&B and sat in a small candle-lit converted barn on beanbags, each of us clutching blankets and hot-water bottles kindly provided by our hostess. My hot-water bottle was introduced to me as 'Lambie' because it had a fluffy white cover.

The date

There is an art is setting the right date. People with young children will not want to be away from home during school holidays. Most organizers will avoid obvious holiday periods such as August or Christmas but if you do not have school-age children yourself, you may be oblivious to half terms and then find that after you have booked a venue and paid the deposit, many of your participants regretfully report that they will be on leave that week. It is easy to check these dates on the Internet. A colleague and I ran an event in Cairo for a British organization. It had not occurred to either of us or to our UK-based client that the date fell within Ramadan until it was too late to change. We then had the discomfort of knowing that half of our group were fasting during the day with all its attendant privations and the non-Muslim half felt guilty at eating normally while their hungry colleagues looked on.

Food and drink

Accepting food and drink is one of the ways that human awkwardness is defused but it needs to be the right food and drink. Find out in advance what special requirements people have. The list may include people who are diabetic and have to eat at frequent intervals, vegetarians, vegans, people who hate fat, hate carbs or have allergies and food intolerances (see Figure 4.1). Let the caterer know in good time.

Figure 4.1
Source: © Steven Appleby (2006c).

Cheap food will convey that whoever is sponsoring the meeting believes that saving a few pounds on food matters more than the needs of the participants. Equally, over-elaborate food may create unease. When the BBC owned a conference centre in Worcestershire, part of it was run as a 5-star hotel. It was not uncommon for participants to complain about what they felt was the oppressive pomposity of the service at dinner. 'Why do they have to cover every plate with those dome things and then do all the melodrama of whipping them off?' 'Why do the puddings have all that silly decoration?'

After a few days of this, there was always a small cohort of people who sneaked off to the local pub for fish and chips instead. Plenty of water is essential but iced tap water is as good as anything in fancy bottles. I always ask for a fruit bowl as well as biscuits for mid-morning and afternoon breaks. Note that the lack of such accompaniments to tea and coffee is always taken as a sign of being a cheapskate by groups and they are right: the resentment it creates makes it a false economy. A heavy sit-down lunch in a formal restaurant will leave people feeling bloated and sleepy and also take far too long to serve and eat, whatever the venue says about its speediness. A light buffet is far better. Resist any suggestion that alcohol might be included with lunch. I still remember with horror a day I facilitated for an organization with a cheerful, frisky culture and which mostly employed young people. It was in the hospitality sector so naturally they liked to be hospitable. There was copious free wine and beer available at lunchtime and no useful work was done that afternoon.

Equipment

Experienced facilitators like to carry their own emergency kit of essential gear. This is because venues cannot be relied upon to have the basics. For instance, people who do not write on flip charts themselves often do not realize that felt-tip pens do not last long, so the pens they provide may have died long since. They also do not know that thin, round-ended pens are useless and that no one can read green or brown from a distance. Consider assembling and taking with you: a decent set of black and red pens, Blu-tack, masking tape and Post-it notepads. Ask for two portable flip charts and refuse to accept the wall-mounted versions because they are hopeless, always too high for short people and in the wrong part of the room. I prefer the low-tech flexibility of a flip chart but there are times when only PowerPoint will do. Check whether projectors are included in the price and what IT help is available. Internet access and Wi-Fi are expected as standard now though you may want to check out easy access to printing and photocopying. The larger the group, the more important it may be to consider amplification for yourself and group members. For methodologies such as Open Space and other large group interventions (p. 98) microphones are normally essential but ensure that technical support is available on the day: this is not an area for DIY.

The room itself

A room that is too big, too small, badly lit, too hot or too cold will get in the way of what you want to achieve. Whenever you can, check out the room in advance. Long thin rooms pose particular horrors as they invariably mean tennis-match talking and there is no easy way to prevent the people at the edges from feeling excluded. If the room is unsuitable, do everything you can to change it. Always get to the venue at least an hour and a half early. My experience is that despite clear instructions to the contrary, venues almost invariably lay a room out in boardroom style. This is often a large solid block of tables that may be far too formal and a lot too big for the purpose. If the room itself cannot be changed, it is usually possible to rearrange the furniture so that you create the climate you want. In hotels, especially, those apparently solid-looking tables can be quickly dismantled by willing porters. If the porters are unavailable or unwilling then get early-arriving participants to help you do the furniture-moving.

Arranging the seating

There are a number of choices here: the boardroom (see Figure 4.2); the café tables arrangement; the U shape and the circle or octagon. Very occasionally you may have to use a lecture shape if you find that you are landed with a tiered lecture theatre with fixed seating. This is the ultimately non-participative layout where the only person with an easy eye line to everyone is the one at the podium. The more barriers you put in the way of people's eye lines, the less participation there is likely to be.

Furniture can be a difficulty where, for instance, the solid table of the boardroom layout will make it harder for people to speak in a candid and friendly way and people at the corners will find it difficult to get into the discussion. Many boardroom shapes are long thin rectangles rather than squares, thus suggesting a 'top' and 'bottom', with resultant differences in assumed status. Also, tables literally form a barrier.

Circular 'café'-style tables seating 4–8 people are often a creative solution for a big group (see Figure 4.3). This will facilitate small group work, but will also create problems over eye lines and acoustics if you want to facilitate large group discussion. Some people may also feel that the tables are too reminiscent of primary school – or a night club.

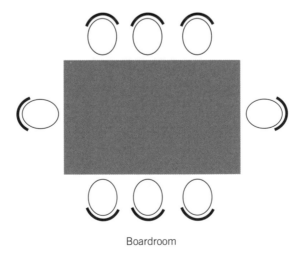

Boardroom

Figure 4.2

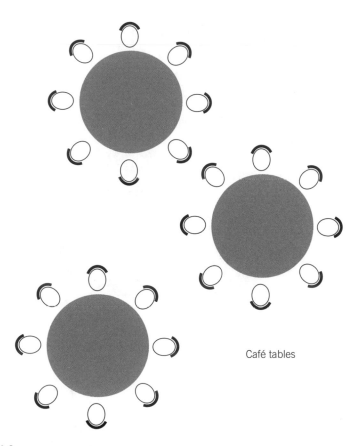

Café tables

Figure 4.3

A U shape has advantages if, for instance, you or anyone else wishes to give a presentation where it will be an advantage to walk into the middle of the 'U' (see Figure 4.4). The eye lines are also reasonably good with this layout, though not as good as with a circle.

A circle or octagon is probably the ideal shape for most facilitated discussions (see Figure 4.5). A circle without any furniture can feel threatening to people as the whole of their bodies are on show at all times. However, where you want to get at real feelings, this is often a good choice for this very reason – there is no hiding place.

An octagonal table that allows people to conceal some of their bodies and also gives opportunities for writing may be a good compromise for small groups. A circle gets unwieldy if there are more than 14 people in it. The space in the centre becomes enormous in order to accommodate everyone. You may then feel you have to have a double circle. This will make it harder for people

U shape

Figure 4.4

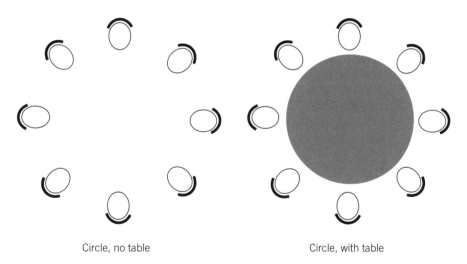

Circle, no table

Circle, with table

Figure 4.5

in the second row to join in. The café-style version is often better for a big group.

As a facilitator, you have more than enough to worry about without having to wrestle the room. Always do what you can to influence the choice of venue and, once there, to improve the environment – it can make a real difference to the outcome.

5   Vital skills

Some problems are so complex that you have to be highly intelligent and well informed just to be undecided about them.

(Dr Laurence J. Peter, author)

As a leader, I have always endeavored to listen to what each and every person in a discussion had to say before venturing my own opinion. Oftentimes, my own opinion will simply represent a consensus of what I heard in the discussion. I always remember the axiom: a leader is like a shepherd. He stays behind the flock, letting the most nimble go out ahead, whereupon the others follow, not realizing that all along they are being directed from behind.

(Nelson Mandela, statesman)

When facilitation is done well, like any complex expertise, it looks seamless – you simply cannot see the joins. However, in this chapter my aim is to take apart some of the vital components of the skill. In practice, you will use them together, but to learn their secrets they have to be studied apart.

Building trust

A facilitated event has to feel safe. Participants have to feel safe with each other and with you. Some anxiety is probably always present in the group and your role is to diminish this as quickly as possible. People may, for instance, be anxious about whether they will be accepted, they may worry about whether they can follow what is going on, may dread embarrassing conflicts being laid bare, or they may fear exposure through looking incompetent.

When you do a lot of facilitating, it is easy to forget how all-pervading such anxiety can be. When I ran a training department, we had regular away-days. I made it a policy that everyone in the department was invited, including our excellent administrators, several of them rather young and certainly more junior than others in the team. I was astonished before the second such day to be approached by a deputation from this group begging to be allowed not to attend. Why? Because they found the whole thing 'stressful' and felt 'out of their depth'. One person told me that she lay awake for a whole night before the previous event, paralysed by the anxiety that I would ask her to say something.

There are a number of ways that you can help to build trust and to take the edge off people's fears. Most importantly, you have to model trustful behaviour yourself. There is no place for sarcasm or put-downs. Never rubbish another department, client or person who is not there. Never, ever, betray the confidentiality of another group by gossiping about them. The group may not react outwardly if you do, but inwardly they will be thinking, 'what's he/she going to say about us after this?'

Listening with respect

Listening seems easy but it is also easy to get it wrong, as these facilitators ruefully observe:

> I realised that I had let an hour and a half go by without speaking at all. The discussion was carrying on without me. I'd got distracted and totally lost the thread of what people were saying.

> I started to offer opinions on the topic under discussion. The client frowned warningly at me but I didn't really see it. A few minutes later he said in front of the group, 'I think our facilitator has forgotten her promise of neutrality'.

Facilitation is fundamentally about respect for participants. Respect means being able to listen by suspending judgement. When we do not listen, the usual reason is because we believe we already know. When you facilitate you listen from careful ignorance. Your mind is open. You listen without feeling the need to criticize, advise, argue, persuade or collude. It means showing all the time that you accept participants.

In practice, there are hundreds of ways of communicating non-acceptance. Table 5.1 shows some of the verbal ones.

Real listening is hard work. Most of us do half or even quarter listening a lot of the time. We do pretend listening – 'yes, go on, I'm listening', while our minds are occupied with something else.

There are also innumerable other ways of communicating disrespect, all of which get in the way of genuine listening when you are a facilitator:

Ignoring the significance of language

Facilitator: How did the pilot project go?
Group member: Not bad. It all worked quite well.
Facilitator: Oh, good. So let's look at how you could incorporate . . .

Here the facilitator has missed the significance of the group member's lack-lustre language *quite well*. Another version of the same thing is when facilitators replace the words used by group members with words of their own that subtly alter their meaning.

Compulsive explaining

The facilitator loves to explain pet theories, tell stories about other clients.

Being wedded to your hypothesis

Here the facilitator jumps to conclusions far too soon or else sees everything in terms of oversimplified version of problems other clients have brought; for example, 'business processes', 'work–life balance' and so on.

Taking sides

The facilitator is unaware of his or her own bias and is unconsciously rewarding some opinions and people more than others; for instance, giving the most senior person most airtime, or favouring female over male participants – or vice versa; offering comment and implicit praise to some people and not others; for instance, with comments such as 'that's a good idea'.

Saying	Effect conveyed to the other person
Don't worry	Trivializes your concern
I hear what you say	The speaker is not listening
Don't you think you should . . .?	The speaker is, annoyingly, giving you their best advice
Can we move on here to the really important issues?	Impatience – the speaker's concerns are more important
Oh dear. [Silence]	This really is embarrassing; you shouldn't have embarrassed us both
There's nothing to get upset about	You are silly for getting upset – a more sensible person would have remained calm

Table 5.1

Psychologizing and interpreting

Attributing simple behaviours to some past trauma (*I can see that this reminds you of that time when the team nearly went under*) or underlying significance when in fact they are just simple behaviours.

The wish to reform the client group

Group member: We're all so tired and stressed all the time.

Facilitator: Yes, well I've mentioned before that I have a colleague who specializes in stress reduction and I really think you should commission her . . .

The experience of really being listened to is a powerful one. The Bill Clinton character in the cheeky and (initially) anonymously published (see Klein, 1996) novel *Primary Colors*[1] about the early stages of his first presidential campaign is described as doing 'aerobic listening' that has an overwhelming impact on the people he is with, much as the real Clinton is reputed to do. One character is described as 'staggering under it' (p. 2).

> He was in heavy listening mode, the most aggressive listening the world has ever known: aerobic listening. It is an intense, disconcerting phenomenon – as if he were hearing quicker than you can get the words out, as if he were sucking the information out of you.

Real listening cannot be faked. To do it you have to be what is called 'fully present' for the other person. Your aim is empathy, a non-judgemental state that aims to understand the other person and to get as far inside their mind as you possibly can. You want to know what they really think and feel. To achieve it, you have to listen with exquisite attention. This means first of all banishing your own concerns, opinions and judgements. If you do not these will get in the way of truly hearing the other person. Real listening is about being prepared to be influenced rather than waiting for your turn to speak in the conversation. It also means avoiding interpreting: listening does not mean that you are busy diagnosing, or creating a theory in your head about what the person is saying. Your energy, rather, goes into truly trying to hear them. You will also be listening for content: giving your whole attention to the other person. Mentally note the themes and ideas in what the person is saying. Be sparing about voicing any associations these set off for you. Wanting to voice them could come from your own wish to impress or to discharge some of your own anxiety. Self-edit these responses unless you are certain they will help the person and the group. Finally, listen and observe for the other messages. This will include people's posture, eye contact, facial expression and colour, the emotion in or behind the words and what has *not* been said – the messages that are being given by implication.

Summarizing

I notice that inexperienced facilitators often lose control of the discussion. They intervene less and less for fear of seeming rude or of saying the wrong thing. The result is that the discussion swirls on around them and eventually the group just ignores them. The longer you let this go on, the more likely it is that you will become invisible and therefore be unable to do your job as facilitator.

Summarizing gives you a respectful way of getting back into the conversation. Places to summarize will include:

- The discussion has continued without a word from you for more than 10 minutes.
- You are puzzled and confused. If you are, the chances are that the group will be too.
- There is a high level of emotion in the room.
- A bewildering range of options has been suggested.
- The group is in effect queuing to speak – no one is listening to anyone else.

If you do nothing else as a facilitator but summarize, you will probably still have done a valuable job. First, it shows that you are listening because you cannot summarize accurately unless you have been listening properly. Second, it reassures participants that someone is keeping track of things. This is particularly important where there has been a period of intense and rambling discussion. Equally importantly, it keeps you in the frame and emphasizes your role.

Genuine summarizing
Genuine summarizing represents the main themes of the discussion.

- It does not contain any judgements of your own – you can give these later if appropriate.
- It is authentically a summary and not a long saunter through the same territory.
- It uses the language employed by participants, not your own.
- It does not attempt to impose neat conclusions; in fact, it is often most useful when the discussion has included a great deal of confusion and conflicting opinion:

> So if I've got this right, X, you said you believe . . . and Y then maintained that . . . was true while Z, I think you said that . . .

- It ends with a question – have I got that right? Or, 'Is that a fair summary?'

Some useful summarizing phrases are as follows:

- It feels to me that it would be useful to summarize where we've got to here . . . There seem to be three or four main views that people have been putting forward . . .
- Can I check that I've really understood the points you're making here? What you feel is that . . .
- So to summarize the discussion so far . . .
- Or even the very brief, *so you feel angry about this?*

Two words of warning: facilitating is often about keeping things open rather than closing them down. The duty to summarize is about helping the group keep track of its options not necessarily to find solutions. Often your role will be about preventing a false consensus developing. It may be a lot better to encourage the group to live with ambiguity than to seek to close things down too soon.

It is possible to overdo summarizing. If you do it too frequently the group may notice it as a 'technique' and become irritated. I once watched an inexperienced and nervous facilitator deliver summaries roughly every three minutes until the group became exasperated, eventually begging her to refrain.

Interrupting

To summarize you may have to interrupt and the two techniques are often profitably used together. Every group contains a member who will maunder on at a moment's notice. Sometimes this is the most senior person present. Facilitators have to overcome their learned politeness here. It is far worse to let the maunderer maunder than to risk the apparent rudeness of interrupting. Signs that you need to interrupt include:

- someone has been holding the floor for at least four minutes without the assent of the group
- you notice that the rest of the group has switched off or is looking bored and irritated
- you are feeling irritated or bored yourself

- you are confused about what is being said
- the person talking is repeating something they have already said several times
- the discussion is taking a circular route; your sense is that no progress is being made
- the discussion seems to be going off on a tangent

Ask yourself whether it is in the group's interests to interrupt. If the answer is *yes*, or *probably*, then you must.

Here's how to do it:

- Trust your instinct that an interruption is needed.
- Wait for a pause for breath in whoever is speaking and lean forward sharply and noticeably.
- If the speaker still does not get it, hold up a hand, palm out.
- Ask permission to interrupt or just announce that you are doing it; for instance:
  I'm going to stop you there, X . . . .
  Can I interrupt you, X?
- Check with the group *always* on whether it is useful or not for the discussion or for the person holding the floor to continue on whatever lines are being followed, explaining your own assumptions and thinking.
  I'm pausing you there, X, because I'm not certain whether it's useful for the discussion to continue along these lines because [and you give your reasons]. *What do you all think?*
- It is also often necessary to combine an interruption with a summary.
  So, X, I'm going to interrupt you here. So to summarize, what you believe is [then you give the summary].

Clarifying

It is not the case that everyone who attends an event is wonderfully articulate. Some people are chronically nervous because of the unwelcome exposure they feel at speaking in public. Others may betray their typically jumbled thoughts in incomplete sentences, hesitations while they search for the elusively right word, or just blush and stop abruptly. You can help here in various ways. The easiest is just to encourage with nods and smiles. Additionally, you can prompt with phrases like:

That sounds interesting – what else would you like to add?

If there is uncertainty about which of two options a person is endorsing, ask, by saying:

Could you just clarify for us which idea you feel is stronger here?

A summary using the person's own vocabulary, ending as I have described above with a question to check on its accuracy, is also helpful.

Signposting

It is easy to ignore the usefulness of this simple technique. It means that wherever possible you label each of your interventions as a way of signalling your intentions. This removes ambiguity, shapes the group's expectations and makes it easier for them to hear what you say. Such signposts may take different forms. For instance, they may name the technique you are going to employ by asking a question such as, *May I try a summary here?* This is especially useful if the intervention you are going to make is potentially unconventional or alarming; for instance, offering feedback or interrupting. They may also signal a link from one part of the discussion to another such as, *It seems as if we are moving now from the discussion about causes to the problem-solving stage.* Or they may show that you intend to offer affirmation to group members, *So as X said in the point he made so powerfully earlier on today . . .* You may also want to flag the possibility that someone in the group may disagree with some firmly held opinion: *So X has said . . . but I'm wondering what other viewpoints there might be here?*

Matching

As a facilitator, you need to be in rapport with the group. You will create rapport by careful matching – of their body language, mood and language. Many facilitators do this naturally, but others have to learn it as a conscious skill, including knowing when and how to take the risk of deliberate mismatching. I work with one very skilled facilitator who uses mismatching to excellent effect. For instance, we were working with one group that was apparently full of sober, serious young people in the financial services sector. My colleague told me later that he was dismayed at what felt like the 'dull' mood in the room. After a few moments of solemnity himself, he then began some rapid-fire jokes and active moving about the room. It worked and soon the group was smiling, sitting up and generally looking about 100 per cent more lively than they had 10 minutes earlier. But this was a high-risk strategy. Less experienced facilitators would move more cautiously from solemnity to high energy.

Questioning

Skilled facilitators have a range of questioning techniques, all of them useful when you want to draw out a response and encourage people to explore and explain their ideas.

Open questions

This is the most basic kind of useful question. An open question obliges the other person to respond with a sentence or phrase rather than a single 'yes' or 'no'. So asking, 'Have you finished what you wanted to say?' invites a very different response from an open version, 'What else would you like to say?'

The most useful words here are:

> What . . .?
> How . . .?

This is because they typically produce a fuller response. Other useful phrases to draw people out include:

> Tell me . . .
> Could you say more about . . .?

Questions beginning 'why' need to be used with care. 'Why' questions can often sound like an interrogation and may lead to a defensive answer that intellectualizes or rationalizes. Rephrasing the question as a 'what' question will often produce a more interesting response. So, for example, 'What was in your mind when you did that?' is more likely to get a full response than 'Why did you do that?' When you ask a 'Why did you . . .?' kind of question, the respondent will often reply, 'I don't know' – end of conversation. Similarly, *when* and *where*, although in theory open questions typically produce a factual response and do not necessarily move the discussion on.

Keep your questions short. A single question no more than 12 words long is ideal. Double or even worse, triple questions just confuse the listener. For instance, *What started this trend and is it likely to continue?* This is two separate questions, both of which could be important, so take them one at a time.

Moving the discussion on

Closed questions have their place. 'Have we exhausted that topic?' implies that the answer is 'yes' and will allow you to move on quickly. These are useful when your sense is that you are approaching the beginning or end of some phase of the discussion. These questions expect the answer yes or no. Examples would be:

> I'm noticing a bit of restlessness in the room. Is it time for a break?

> Have we bottomed that issue now?

> Should we move on?

> Shall we make a start?

> So our next topic is X. A, would you like to introduce it?

Linking questions or statements are also useful here. Links combine a brief summary of the discussion that has just happened with a look forward to the next section. Here is an example:

> *So in this part of the discussion we've looked at how the pressures on the business are affecting it in a number of ways* (you then briefly enumerate them) *and our plan now is to look in more detail at each of these. Is that OK?*

For daily examples of how to do this elegantly, examine any live discussion programme on TV or radio. Broadcasters call these links 'segues', meaning a technique of sliding seamlessly from one topic to another by making a link between them.

Language

'Clean' language

The expert facilitator is a close observer of the language used by the group.

This concept has been made more elegant and straightforward by Neuro Linguistic Programming (NLP) enthusiasts, based on the work of David Grove, a therapist who developed his approach in the 1980s and 1990s through work with war veterans and survivors of abuse. Grove published little in his lifetime but his ideas have been made accessible by others, including Wendy Sullivan and Judy Rees (2008). Judy Rees describes it on the Businessballs website (businessballs.com) as *the natural language of the mind, particularly the unconscious mind.* When you employ it, people feel understood at a profound level because what they want to communicate, so often presented elliptically, is made clear to everyone, including themselves.

Clean language is about spotting and working with the metaphors and similes we use constantly: there has been research suggesting, for instance, that we may sometimes use as many as six such constructions per minute in every-day speech. When you look out for these expressions, they are indeed common.

> I don't know how we're going to manage the *burden* of these redun-dancies. The legal process is such a *maze*. It makes me feel we're *wading through treacle*. The financial side of it is a *nightmare* and the people side is going to be appalling. I've always hated these conversations – feel as if I'm personally *killing* the person.
>
> (Team member at awayday)

Here, there is no actual burden, maze, wading, treacle, nightmare or killing. The speaker has used words that bring vividness, complexity and directness to convey feeling. When you probe for the meaning underpinning such words you will find that each individual brings a different interpretation, and this is where clean language is so revealing.

Essential propositions

- The facilitator notices group members' language: as well as similes and metaphors this can include 'nominalizations' – abstract nouns, adjectives and verbs that have no meaning without behaviour attached to them. Examples include: *happiness, modernization, opti-mism* and *assertiveness*.
- Using group members' exact words creates rapport.
- The facilitator uses phrases that are as far as possible 'cleansed' of any of their own presuppositions, interpretations and assumptions.
- The facilitator draws attention to any of the non-verbal signals that accompany group members' words; for example a raised arm, a hand on heart, a jiggling foot, without making any of the popular inter-pretations; for example that crossed arms means defensiveness.
- The facilitator directs group members' attention to their own ges-tures, metaphors and language and asks them to interpret them through expanding on them.
- Clean language works best when it is focused on the positive so, for instance, some of the best uses of the technique are to ask what the person wants more of, rather than a deficit or problem focus where you would ask what the person wants less of.
- Doing this enables the group member – and the group – to understand their own 'perceptual world'; that is, their own assumptions, blocks and barriers.

Unclean language: an example

Group member: This team is toxic.
Facilitator: So how could it be less poisonous?

In this example, the facilitator substitutes her own adjective and also assumes that the group member wants a less toxic environment before taking the time to understand what *toxic* means to the speaker. The hidden instruction is that a less toxic environment is desirable and that the group member should find it immediately.

Exploring what such a vivid metaphor actually means will lead to a far richer discussion. In this example, a team was struggling to come to terms with its own negative patterns of behaviour.

Clean language: a real example

Group member: This team is toxic.
Facilitator: And what kind of toxic is toxic?
Group member: It's a virus.
Facilitator: And what kind of a virus is that?
Group member: It's rampant, gets everywhere, spoils everything, infects people who were healthy previously, the temperature gets raised [Group member places her hand on her forehead]
Facilitator: [Copies group member's hand movement briefly] And when this happens and people get infected and the temperature gets raised what happens next?
Group member: We shut down, we retreat, we moan.
Facilitator: And then?
Group member: We get paralysed. But we need to search for the cure.
Facilitator: If you did search for the cure what would be happening?
Group member: We'd see that we've inflicted the virus on ourselves and we'd need a vaccine to stop it happening again!
Facilitator: And if you had that vaccine, what would be happening?
Group member: We would start by being ruthlessly honest with ourselves and each other.

How to do it

- The facilitator slows down his or her speech.
- There is an implied sense of wonder and curiosity in the way the questions are asked.

- The group members' idiosyncratic emphases and pronunciation are matched.
- Only the group members' language, metaphors and similes are used.

Useful phrases

And what kind of < > is that < >?

And where does that < > come from?

And that's like . . . what?

And what happens next?

And is there anything else about < >?

Tell me more about < >

What does < > mean for you?

If you had < > what would be happening?

Encouraging people to be specific

Many of us are vague in our language, often using comparisons and generalizations unthinkingly as a way of providing emphasis and drama to what we say. As with clean language, this process clarifies vagueness to the point where it becomes specific and therefore productive, see Table 5.2.

Allowing silence

In social life, silence is difficult to tolerate and most of us will rush in to cover even a short silence three or four seconds long. In a group this is not always beneficial. One of the helpful things you can do as a facilitator is to make it possible to tolerate silence for longer than is usual. Sometimes in a facilitated discussion, someone will say something that contains a painful degree of self-disclosure or strong feeling. The group's reaction may be silence. Do not assume that this silence means that 'nothing' is happening. At one level nothing is being said, but at another the silence may convey people's confusion, pity, fellow-feelings, anger – the range is enormous. There may be a feeling that the silence is hard to bear. But who is finding it hard? It may not be hard for the person who has spoken. Keeping the silence may often be a better way of demonstrating concern and acceptance.

Silence will also allow more reflection from everyone, including you.

Where it is appropriate, I might quietly reassure a group at this juncture that silence is fine.

Statement	Facilitator's follow-up technique and question
A comparison of some kind; for instance: 'This is the worst department I've ever been in'	Surface the comparison, ask 'worst in what way?' or 'Worse than what, specifically?'
'Our customer service is better than anyone else's'	Ask for specifics; for example, 'How, specifically, is your customer service better?'
Generalizations; for instance: 'We always answer the phone in a sloppy way' 'Everyone thinks appraisal is a waste of time'	Challenge the generalization by gently saying, 'Always – do you really mean that?' Or 'What are the exceptions?' 'Does everyone actually think that – who might disagree here?'
Bald assertions, for instance: 'I don't like the way this organization is going'	Ask for a specific example; for example: 'Could you tell us what specifically you don't like?'
Statement of implied rules that indicate firmly held beliefs; for instance: 'We should know exactly what our work programme is' 'I must have advanced warning of changes in the plans' 'Can'ts' may represent particularly strongly held self-limiting beliefs; for instance: 'I can't change the fact that I have to work long hours'	Surface the implied rule and ask what the result would be of changing their beliefs; for example: 'What would happen if you didn't know exactly what your work programme was?' Alternatively, ask for clarification on what holding this belief is doing for the person; for example: 'What would having advanced warning do for you?' Challenge the belief by asking: 'What would need to change for you to alter your view here?' 'What's stopping you working a shorter day?'

Table 5.2

Observing

A lot of the skill in facilitating is in constant discreet watching. Who hasn't spoken for a while? Who is looking sleepy? Who is sitting on the edges of their chairs? Who wants to speak? Who constantly interrupts other people?

Observation means looking with empathy and care. It also means looking for the small clues that suggest someone is holding something back, and then perhaps coaxing out what needs to be said. The elements to look for here are:

- evenness of contribution generally in the group
- proportion of men to women speaking or juniors to seniors
- levels of energy in the group: posture, gesture, volume and amount of speech
- people's emotional state

The so-called 'lighthouse effect' is helpful here: keep sweeping the room with your eyes, engaging each person in brief eye contact. This keeps everyone in the frame and also gives you the opportunity to see what is happening.

There are common patterns and tendencies that you can look out for:

- The more senior people are, the more they will talk.
- Men will talk more than women and will volunteer more readily for informal leadership roles such as reporting back on small group discussions.
- Men will make assertions while women will frame their thoughts as questions.
- Ping-pong dialogues can develop – typically between you and one or two other members of the group, or between the most senior person and a select group of others in the group.
- The person sitting directly in your eye line will have the most encouragement to speak and the people sitting immediately to your right and left will have the worst eye lines so will tend to say least.
- People will colonize one seat, leaving their coats and papers on it and returning to that place after every break.
- Physical distances – in other words, how people place their chairs – subtly increase between people when they are feeling defensive and uncertain and decrease when they are feeling safe.
- People sit next to those with whom they feel they have most in common. So, for instance, you may notice that all the younger men are sitting together, or all the people who do the same job or who work in the same department.

You can best manage these common phenomena by:

- being aware of them – if you are unaware, you cannot do anything about them

- raising the group's awareness of them
- breaking up ping-pong dialogue where you see it developing by saying something like, 'I think this is getting to be too much of a dialogue, here. Let's see who else would like to speak'. Where the ping-pong involves you, make a point of not replying to a comment from a group member and leaving a pause so that another member of the group speaks instead. Alternatively, say, 'What do other people think here?' and look around the group
- manipulating the seating. For instance, you can ask a quieter person to sit opposite you and the noisiest person to sit by your side. You can break the 'colonizing' pattern by changing where you sit yourself, or by suggesting to the group that they might like to change where they sit. In longer facilitated events, as people become more comfortable and feel safer, this process happens naturally

Giving feedback

This skill takes courage. It arises directly out of the principle that working in the moment is important (p. 26). The words *feedback* and *criticism* are used in common speech interchangeably but they are not actually synonyms. Feedback may be positive or negative and is given entirely for the benefit of the receiver. Its purpose is generous because it is developmental. It is specific, descriptive and about behaviour. Criticism may also be positive when used in the context of a written review of a play or film, but it normally carries a negative connotation. Often offered angrily, it is also vague and generalized, coming across as an attack on the whole person, making it highly likely that the message will be rejected immediately. In many organizations, people are encouraged to criticize. It is seen as dynamic, intellectually sharp, daring and sophisticated. I well remember my own shock as a naïve young adviser on adult education to the BBC on attending my first TV production department meeting where the head of department urged people on by crying, *'Not enough shredding, people! Not enough shredding!'* The violence of the metaphor was striking: it encouraged harsh criticism of colleagues' programmes, dressed up as plain speaking or witticism. Privately, these meetings were held to be unbearable because of the fear and embarrassment they induced. When people did join in they often confessed to shame afterwards and apologized to the colleague who had been the target.

How the group behaves with each other in the room will give you many opportunities for feedback, as will how they behave with you. If you have gathered data before the event, you will also need to offer feedback on the themes that have emerged.

Why is it then that so few facilitators employ this powerful technique? The most obvious reason is that we are all afraid of it, whether we are the giver or the receiver. As a receiver of feedback, you may typically exaggerate the dangers; for instance, you might be afraid that you would hear confirmation of your own worst fears about yourself, and that if you did hear such confirmation, you might fall apart because your self-image, maintained only by the most fragile edifice, would fracture irreparably. You may also associate feedback with criticism, not with appreciation, thus adding to the dread. Similarly, many people have been brought up with such fierce internal voices of condemnation that they cannot hear the positives in any feedback they are offered, and only pay attention to the negatives. As a giver of feedback, when you share these fears you may hesitate to offer it. Might the recipient be angry, or even worse, might they weep with shame or hurt? And if they did, how would you cope with the aftermath, in you and in them?

All these negative fantasies have a root in reality. To give feedback you have to know that it needs exquisite tuning in intention and delivery. It helps to remind yourself that feedback can change people's perceptions and that once perceptions change, behaviour has a chance of changing too. You offer it from a position of strength because you are outside the group and your lack of investment in a continuing relationship with them will be what gives you freedom to be candid.

You must also be certain that you have permission to offer the feedback, that it is needed and that you know how to deliver it. I watched an inexperienced facilitator get this embarrassingly wrong on a programme for senior doctors where, only 30 minutes into the day, she announced that she was going to give the group feedback, then informed them of how *impressed* she was by their *openness to learning* – implied but not actually said, '*unlike the rest of your profession*'. Since everyone in the room was already a distinguished educator and she a jobbing freelance, this felt false, naïve and patronizing to say the least. Most probably it simply broke the rule of keeping your mouth firmly shut when what you have to say is more about you and your needs – in this case perhaps to try earning their approval by offering them praise – than for the benefit of the group.

A safe and powerful way to frame feedback

The essence of real feedback is that it is descriptive and not evaluative, specific not generalized. You describe the behaviour you have seen, based on verifiable facts, not opinion as the following example shows:

> A facilitator notices that the group seems to have a habit of interrupting each other.

Non-feedback: the wrong way to do it

You are a very noisy raggle-taggle group in your discussions aren't you! You like talking over each other!

Comment: this is a generalization: implies that the group is always noisy. The comments are also evaluative because *noisy* and *raggle-taggle* imply negatives. The word 'noisy' is vague and does not have any behaviour attached to it. The facilitator has also added an interpretation. She believes she can read the motivation of the group members in interrupting each other. The chances are that this clumsily given 'feedback' will be rejected and will also be perceived as rude.

Feedback alternative: the right way to do it

May I offer you some feedback? I noticed that about three minutes ago when we were discussing topic X, several people [you name them] *started talking at once. The same thing happened about 10 minutes earlier. What I noticed was that when this happened, other people glanced around the table to see who was actually speaking, I know I did and got a bit bemused at that point! What I'm wondering is how typical this is of your discussions? What do you think?*

Comment: this is genuine feedback, given respectfully but straightforwardly. It is based on close observation and on factually observed behaviour. It does not contain judgement or interpretation. The facilitator also owns her own opinion – that she felt bemused. She asks what links there might be to the group's typical behaviour and invites a reply. Feedback like this may not always be comfortable to hear but is rarely rejected because it is so palpably based on evidence and will virtually always produce a thoughtful pause and valuable discussion.

Here is the protocol in seven easy steps:

1 Face up to and overcome your reluctance to give feedback.
2 Ask permission to offer the feedback.
3 Describe what you have seen, concentrating on the factual details of behaviour, using a phrase such as *What I noticed . . .*, or *I observed that when . . .* or *I sensed that. . . .* Do not evaluate the behaviour. For instance, saying, *X, you looked disengaged* is an evaluation and an interpretation. Instead, describe what you have actually seen and ask the person themselves to explain their motivation: *X, I noticed you pushed your chair away from the table at that point. I wonder what was going on for you then?*

4   Describe the impact on you.
5   Ask what links there are to whatever the issue or problem is, beginning, *I'm wondering . . .*
6   Ask for comments from the group.
7   Agree how to take things forward.

Although feedback, as in the example above, is commonly used to address a negative, it is equally powerful when used to reinforce a positive. Examples might be where a group or individual is experimenting successfully with new behaviour. Feedback then recognizes the change and improvement.

Teaching groups the feedback protocol is also valuable: ideally, you should not be the only person in the room who has this duty or who possesses the skill. For instance, it is a vital part of getting the most from process reviews.

Using process review

Most facilitated events benefit from asking the group to review its own process – its patterns of interaction, the way the spoken and unspoken feelings affected what happened. You may want to do this at brief regular intervals throughout the event, or just at the end. Groups have no difficulty in answering the questions and typically contribute shrewd, insightful and thoughtful comments. The difficulty, if there is one, lies in saying what is not normally said out loud. Some useful questions to ask are:

What have the patterns been here?

Who has spoken most? How did you feel about that?

Who has spoken least?

What explains these patterns?'

What has the emotional temperature of the discussion been?

What was going through your minds when [some difficulty or conflict] was being discussed?

What learning has there been here for you as a group about how you operate?

Whose questions and contributions have been the most helpful in X or Y part of the discussion?

Keep any process discussions short by suggesting a discrete time for them and sticking to it. You are not doing group therapy that is in effect one long process review. Where a group has a continuing life outside the event you are facilitating, you can encourage them to adopt a modified form of this proto-col and apply it to their normal meetings, invariably with considerable benefit.

Mechanics

Timekeeping

This is a simple one, but is often forgotten. A group can become involved in a discussion and forget about time. This is their right but in any case it is your role to manage the time. Always sit where you can see a clock without moving your head, or put your watch on a table where you can glance at it frequently. The questions to ask might include:

> *How much more do we have to get through in this session?*
>
> *How far are we making progress in this discussion – I notice we've stayed on it for an hour?*
>
> *Is this phase of the discussion contributing to the group's understanding?*
>
> *Who hasn't spoken recently?*
>
> *Who is looking bored or fidgety?*
>
> *How helpful is it to look at this issue in so much depth?*

Remind the group of time, for example, 'It's now 11.20 and we've spent 20 minutes on this topic. Is it time to move on?' or 'We've got another 10 minutes until the break. Should we stay with this, or get on to the next phase?' The decision about whether to abandon or continue the discussion should be the group's not yours, which is why it is important to make this kind of intervention as a question.

Marshalling

There is often a point on a facilitated event where so much information and so many ideas have been generated that the group begins to feel confused. While you might not be the only person whose responsibility it is to marshal the main themes, you must be one of the people who does. Tactics that I have found helpful here are:

- reducing possible sources of confusion by preparing carefully and getting myself fully briefed well in advance. This is another reason why talking to participants ahead of time is useful – you will have far more sense of what their preoccupations, favourite acronyms and jargon are if you have already spoken to them

- to keep a notebook on my lap and to jot down key words while people are talking
- to remind myself constantly that I am looking for patterns and themes in each session
- to keep summarizing for the group – if I am getting off track, then they will tell me

Recording information

Flip charts and electronic aids are another way of marshalling the flow of the discussion. Recording what people say enables you and them to review it more easily. There are a number of useful tips to pass on here. I like the low-tech flexibility of flip charts because that way I don't have to bother lugging my laptop around or worry about whether there will be a projector along with mystifying instructions about connecting it to my machine. Where flip charts are concerned:

- Do not assume that you have to do all the writing. If you are constantly turning away to write on the flip chart, you cannot scan the group. Also, it can look too school-teachery. If you do not have a co-facilitator, share out this chore among the group. Ask for people whose writing is confident and speedy, and encourage them to note down main points only.
- Keep to lower-case writing (quicker to write and easier to read).
- Use chunky red, blue or black pens.
- Squared paper (not widely available) is easier to work with than blank pages; for example, helps with diagrams and keeping the page neat.
- Do not number any points made as this may convey an inappropriate sense of priority.
- Where you do note down points yourself, make sure you include a verb in each phrase. This will make the meaning a lot clearer, especially if the flip charts are later typed up.
- Wherever you can, get to the flip chart early and prepare instructions or frameworks for sessions well in advance.
- Agree in advance who will be taking responsibility for any flip-charted material and for what will happen to it after the event. It is good practice for flip charts and other notes to be reviewed calmly later and edited down to material that will make sense to people who were there and to people who were not if, indeed, any output is needed at all. This is a client responsibility, not yours.

Powerpoint may be valuable for reporting back on briefing conversations or on the results of other pre-event activity (see p. 56). It has the advantage of being able to provide printed copies as a permanent record. If you are using it, keep the presentation short and each page simple with no more than 50 characters. Avoid clip art illustrations because they are overused and have therefore become clichés.

Note

1   The journalist Joe Klein was quickly unmasked as the author and after several unconvincing denials finally admitted the truth.

6   Facilitator nightmares: what if . . .?

The Chinese use two brushstrokes to write the word crisis. One brush stroke stands for danger, the other for opportunity. In a crisis be aware of the danger but recognise the opportunity.

(John F. Kennedy, US President)

He who never made a mistake never made a discovery.

(Samuel Smiles, author)

General principles

The facilitator role can feel lonely. You can never anticipate exactly what might happen and if things do go wrong, the potential mortification is very public. Many facilitators worry a lot about this. Crises may be major or minor. Some may actually be amusing; for instance, I still smile remembering an event in Zug, Switzerland where the group had teased me by mysteriously hinting at 'an interruption'. We were running the day from a room facing an enclosed artificial lake. As the local church bells struck six, an extraordinary cacophony began: tens of thousands of frogs, all singing along to the bells, so loudly that the whole event had to stop. The group enjoyed my startlement very much. While that was a benign event, the one where a participant suddenly ran out of the room, shouting and inexplicably accusing me of 'unfairness' was not so pleasant.

There are some general principles that it helps to remember.

It is unlikely that any abuse or criticism directed at you is actually personal. It is far more likely to be a reflection of tension in the group but projected on you. If you remember this, it will be easier to stay in a neutral, positive mode. A distinguished facilitator of my acquaintance was running a two-day event for the executive team of a large organization. One of my coaching clients was present at this event. She told me that his generous fee had become known to the group. He was famous for his terse style. It became a private game for the group to count his words and then to calculate how much per word the organization was paying him. What was really going on here? The facilitator was undoubtedly seen as the creature of the detested chief executive who had hired him. People were physically present but mentally absent, playing along sufficiently to give the appearance of participation while actually sniggering with each other privately about what rubbish the whole thing was. Yes, mature, exceptionally well-paid people can still indulge in such childish behaviour rather than doing the grown-up thing of offering their boss direct feedback and challenge.

Do not ever enter into a personal argument with a group member as this is a conflict you cannot win. Do not waste time and energy speculating about people's motives. Constantly express your respect and concern for the group, for instance, by reminding them that your role is to work with them to achieve a positive outcome. Check frequently for feedback from the group about how it is going from their perspective. By showing them that you will not shrivel if such feedback is negative you are doing two things: modelling how to ask for and receive feedback and also encouraging them to offer it without being asked.

Mostly it is better to deal with any offending behaviour overtly during the group sessions. In many group discussions there is concern about 'hidden agendas'. By sticking to the principle of dealing openly with difficulties, you are modelling what it feels and looks like to have unguarded agendas. The biggest single mistake made by inexperienced facilitators is to confuse neutrality on the task issues with neutrality on the process. You are not neutral on process issues: that is the essence of your role. In most of the advice that follows you will see that I advocate intervention. Never hang back where you observe a negative pattern developing.

There are limits to what a facilitator can ever do. Remind yourself that responsibility to take action on the organizational tasks lies with the group and not with you. They own the problems and if they choose not to move forward then they live with the aftermath, not you. You will never know as much about the complexities of the issues as the group and sometimes as the event unfolds, multiple tangles and barriers start to appear. There are some situations where it becomes obvious that the event is a cynical exercise in pretend participation and there is no corrective you can apply. There are also groups where the relationships have reached such high levels of toxicity that a different kind of intervention is needed; most probably one where at least some members of the group should leave it permanently. Facilitation is not the answer to every problem. While it is always properly professional to consider your own responsibility when some apparent disaster happens, equally it is important not to beat yourself up unnecessarily about elements that even the best facilitator in the world could not have affected. Often there is no neat solution and you should accept that some disappointment is part of every facilitator's experience.

Even in an event that apparently ends in failure, there are often longer-term positive outcomes because the process has profitably disturbed the status quo. People may have spoken truthfully to each other for the first time, decisions that have been looming for individuals or for the group may have been accelerated. Often, what has been trying to happen does happen as a result of such an event, even if in the short term it feels as if nothing has changed.

Sometimes you will get things wrong. You will for certain make mistakes because you have misunderstood, have not prepared adequately or because you lack some particular expertise. This goes with the patch. Facilitation is not a baby-level skill and some occasional failure is inevitable. Do not retreat when this happens, nursing your supposed humiliation, believing that you will never get the hang of it. Learn what you can, put it into perspective, move on – and do better next time.

In the ordinary run of a facilitated event, the crises tend to follow predictable patterns and there are plenty of workable solutions. Most of the problems are preventable through careful planning (see Chapter 3) but sometimes it is only possible to do partial or improvised preparation, skimping on the conversations that will give you clues about the traps that could lie ahead. Occasionally, even the best planning could not have prevented the crisis happening. This chapter is about identifying such situations and giving advice about how to deal with them.

Cynicism

Group members have arrived without pens or notebooks. They toy with their mobiles or openly send texts, sometimes to each other, while you and others are talking. They fold their arms, look at the floor, push their chairs awry. You suggest an activity and there is no response. There is muttering, there are sideways looks and rolling eyes.

Never ignore these signs as they will wreck the event if not challenged. I once ran a day for a group of journalists. It was about the introduction of a new appraisal system. About half an hour after we had started, the door burst open and in strolled a wild-looking figure with several rolled up newspapers under his arm. 'Oh, it's Keith!' cried the group, implying that Keith was a rogue and now we would see what was going to happen. Keith's ancient anorak was firmly zipped up; he apologized perfunctorily and sat down, at the same time pushing his chair out of the circle. One of the newspapers was unfolded and he proceeded to read it. The anorak was still zipped up even though the room was warm. Because he had sat in the last chair – and this is always the one closest to the facilitator – he was right next to me. Soon the eyes of everyone in the group were on him and there were the beginnings of suppressed snorts of amusement. I understood that this was a direct challenge. I stopped the discussion and calmly fed back to him what I had seen (I did not feel calm – quite the opposite, felt angry at his rudeness, though reminding myself that I was not the real target of it) and asked how he felt about coming to the day. He looked taken aback at my candour and mumbled something about appraisal systems being 'a load of management bollocks' and not being asked whether or not he wanted to be there, slyly looking at me to see whether I would take offence at the language.

I did not respond to the language but summarized what he had said. I then said evenly that it was not acceptable to me that he continued to behave as he had. He was more than welcome to stay, but he was an adult and could leave at any time. The condition for staying was that he joined in. If at the end of the day he found that it had really been the waste of time he anticipated, then I would be more than pleased to hear his feedback on how to make it more useful. Sheepishly he unzipped the jacket, took it off and decided to stay. I will not say that he joined in with enthusiasm, but his behaviour stayed within acceptable bounds for the rest of the day.

Where several or even most of the group feel resentful, you have no option but to get their feelings out into the open. You cannot expect a good outcome if people are fuming about being there. It is important in such cases not to collude with them about how awful their bosses are to have set up such a meeting without consulting them or of not giving them the option to drop out. You can, however:

- listen carefully to what they have to say
- encourage them to raise the contentious topics with their managers
- ask them what the effect of their resentment and reluctance is likely to be on the activity you have planned for the day
- give them the option to leave

I was working at the BBC during the time a highly unpopular internal market system was being introduced by an equally unpopular senior management regime. Walking down a corridor one day, I heard an excited babble from one of the meeting rooms. The door was open and I glanced in. The room was full of senior managers, some of whom I knew well. One of them came out to talk to me. 'We've just sent a consultant packing!' he crowed. It turned out that the hapless facilitator had tried to start the day and had met mass resistance. The group as a body had demanded the presence of a yet more senior manager 'to answer all the serious objections we have about this project' and had flatly refused to go on until this happened. The facilitator had been sent off to see if he could find the said manager and persuade him to meet the group.

There is truly only one way to deal with resistance and subversion and that is to surface it, name it and then to engage the group in deciding how to deal with it. Where you suspect reluctance you can also ask people to rate their commitment to the event by asking them to fill in a ballot (see Figure 6.1).

When you have charted everyone's rating, discuss what needs to happen to raise commitment to 100 per cent.

Discussion is going round in circles

The discussion begins to sound confusing. You could swear that you have already heard the same point made several times. People's sentences trail off. It is not clear where the discussion is heading – it is still on identifying a problem or is it now at the solutions phase? If you do not know, the chances are the group will not either.

Summarizing (p. 120) can break the block. You say something like 'I've been listening carefully, and what I think I've heard is three different points being made. X made this point (you describe it), Y made this point and Z made this point. Is that a fair summary of what's been said?' Other tactics include:

- Drawing attention to the going round in circles. If you are feeling frustrated by the discussion, the chances are that others will be feeling it too. You could try something like 'we seem to have been stuck at this point for about 10 minutes. Is this useful, or should we move on?'
- Restating the purpose of the topic you are discussing.
- Asking one of the group to restate the problem as they see it.
- Asking what the group feels the best next step in the discussion is.

Discussion seems lifeless

What you do here will depend on your hunch about what the cause is. Some interventions it is worth considering include:

- Drawing attention to the lack of energy, and asking for the group's comments and suggestions.
- Suggesting a break: 'Shall we have a break, or would you rather go on?'
- Having a suite of 'energizers' up your sleeve.

How committed are you at being at this event?

1	2	3	4	5
Wish I wasn't here	Not very keen	Will give it a chance	Pretty committed	100% committed

Figure 6.1   A simple ballot

These might include:

- asking people to change places, and to sit on the opposite side of the room
- opening the windows
- a standing yoga exercise that involves stretching
- a deep breathing demo and practice
- setting up an activity that is done while walking in pairs outside, weather permitting. One way of setting this up is to ask people to line themselves up in leg-length order so that their walking pace is likely to be similar and then to pair up

The undisciplined group: confusing debate with discussion

You are just a short way into the event. Everyone is speaking at once. In fact, some members may be shouting over each other. Some may be pounding the table. It looks and sounds like the House of Commons on one of their more boisterous days.

I was facilitating a day for a management team of seven people. Within half an hour, I noticed that six of the seven were talking at once and for a five-minute period no one, including me, was able to finish a sentence without interruption. Reining them in to look at and then discuss this pattern, I asked them how far this resembled their normal management meetings. This revealed that their discussions were really debates where people quickly took up an extreme position and then defended it. No one listened to anyone else or built on the contributions of others. One result was that decisions rarely got made, or if they did, they were not followed by action. The impact on the whole organization was devastating. Each department acted independently even though cooperation was essential. As a result, their processes were prolonged and inefficient, adding significantly to their costs and often resulting in having to redo work so that its poor quality was not visible to their customers.

When you are an inexperienced facilitator, you may dither about intervening, hoping against hope that such behaviour might improve. I have also known facilitators who beg the group to behave nicely to each other, sounding chronically hesitant and unsure while they do so. Neither of these tactics is desirable.

What works

- Be assertive. Stop the discussion and offer the group feedback (p. 133).

  I notice that for the last five minutes, three different topics have been raised.

  Can I offer you some feedback? In the last part of our discussion, I notice that several people (you give examples) *have been interrupted before they finished their sentences.*

- Ask how typical this is of their usual discussions.
- Ask what the group suggests as a way around the problem. Often people will propose raising their hands to indicate that they want to speak. This will help but only partially, as group members may still not be listening to each other and suggestions may just be followed by counter-suggestions. If so, offer feedback again on what you see and hear happening.
- You will most probably have to intervene frequently as the group defaults to its normal pattern.
- Depending on the situation it may be useful to offer members training in active listening, including techniques such as summarizing, questioning and rephrasing.

Tangent mania – that reminds me . . .

This is another common pattern and equally infuriating to groups, even to members who individually are just as guilty as everyone else of indulging in it. Here is what happens. A topic is under discussion but soon it has whirled off into another topic, then another, then another. Decisions are made – or apparently made – only for a group member to say, 'Actually, I've just thought of something else . . .' and the whole topic is opened again, never to be closed. Commonly, if there is an agenda, it proves extremely difficult to stick to it. People leave feeling confused and depressed – another awful meeting.

Generally speaking there is no malign intent here. One possible explanation is that your preparation has been misleading or incomplete: the agenda is not the most relevant agenda and the tangents are actually the 'real' topics. Check this with the group by asking them directly, again using feedback. If you can then genuinely rule this out, the most likely explanation is that the group has developed this ineffectual pattern of meetings and either is unaware of it, or does not know how to get out of it. Individual members may never have been schooled in meetings' skills and this may be exacerbated by a leader who has never learned how to chair. I worked with one such group where the Chair, actually also the Chair of the organization, had started life as a lawyer and believed that a professional meeting was just like being in court where rules of evidence and natural justice should prevail. Anyone who had an opinion was entitled to air it at great length. Their meetings habitually lasted five hours, when it was clear that the necessary business could easily have been conducted inside 90 minutes.

It is sometimes tempting just to hope for the best, or to hope that a group member will do your job for you and point out the digression. A more common trap is to start eagerly facilitating the tangential discussion. These are not effective tactics.

What to do
Make sure that the agenda has been circulated in advance. Write it on the flip chart on the day and remind people that these are the topics for the event. Check for their agreement that these are the right topics. Alternatively, tell the group in advance that you will be creating the agenda on the spot. There will be one overall question the day is designed to tackle. Remind the group what this is. Give everyone a clutch of Post-it notes and ask them to write one suggested agenda item on each Post-it. With the group's help you then cluster the similar items on a white board and create the agenda on the flip chart. Ask what priority each topic has and tackle the most important first. Track progress during the day, reminding people of how much time is left for remaining items.

If, despite this, you still have problems, the cure is similar to the one I suggest above for overeager debaters.

- Notice the pattern, stop the discussion and offer the group feedback:

  I notice that in the last hour we have had three different topics, none of them ones on our original agenda.

  I notice that there seems to be a pattern – you agree a decision, then a few minutes later the topic has been reopened. (You give an example.) *Personally I'm confused about what has actually been agreed here.*

- Ask whether the tangents are useful. If the answer is yes, then let them continue and facilitate in the usual way but raise the issue of what to drop from the original agenda, reminding the group that time is not elastic.
- If the answer is no, ask the group what they would like you to do to rein the going-off-on-tangents in. They will probably tell you that they want you to challenge them the moment they appear.
- Have a blank flip chart sheet on the wall headed *Holding Bay* and let the person who has raised the topic list it for further discussion at

some other time, but remember to factor in the space for this to happen.

Paralysis by analysis

Here, the group gets ensnared by the complexity of its own analysis and seems unable to move to solutions. Another variant of the phenomenon is when the group seems to have descended into gloom because of the depth of problems its analysis has revealed. The overall solution lies in the design of the day, remembering to plan in some decision-making activities. The most workable answers to the problem will involve having plenty of these ideas up your sleeve so that you can produce them if necessary (p. 92).

You might also try:

- Asking a member of the group to restate the problem or issue: this often serves the function of altering everyone's perspective or helping to reframe the problem.
- Identifying the resources available – what sources of help are available to us? Who haven't we yet consulted who might have something useful to offer?
- Identifying a short-term goal. When your facilitation has helped a group face up to major problems, there can seem so much to do that nothing seems possible. Identifying some small step that can be achieved is often a helpful way to get things going again.
- Identifying what is working well even if only a bit, look at what explains this and ask what can be learned and applied elsewhere.
- Moving the group to a more resourceful state by asking what the ideal solution would be – 'Imagine this problem were solved, what would be going on for you – what would you see, hear and experience?' Now ask, 'What's standing in the way of finding that solution?'
- Breaking the group into pairs. One of the pair represents the problem, the other is consultant. The 'consultant' asks the partner to reframe the problem and then asks the questions above about the ideal solution. The pair swaps round and the whole group then reconvenes to discuss the ideas that were generated.
- Prioritizing. It can also be useful to break the tasks into short-, medium- and long-term goals.
- Brainstorming possibilities without evaluating them until later (see p. 89).
- Changing activities. Leaving a problem hanging while the group does something else can create a breather so that everyone comes back with renewed energy.

A more dramatic technique, which can often work well, is to say to the group, 'We seem to be stuck here. I'd like to suggest something unusual'. You ask everyone to stand up and stand behind their chairs. You then in turn ask each person to use the following formula to make a series of statements:

- What I'm feeling right now is . . . (Watch out for people who give thoughts not feelings and ask them to restate what they have said as a feeling.).
- My suggestion for the group is . . .

This technique can work because it requires people to literally change their physical state and their point of view – they have to stand up and in doing so they see the group from a different perspective. Even more importantly, it allows everyone an equal chance to make suggestions about how to move forward and also allows people to voice their feelings – usually of intense frustration, disappointment or even anger. Legitimizing feelings is often one of the most important things you can do as a facilitator.

Under-contributors

There is no 'rule' of group life that says everyone must contribute in equal measure. However, facilitation is about ensuring that unpopular or unusual opinions are heard and also about guarding against groupthink, so it is important to create opportunities for quieter people to join in. When you have under-contributors you need to distinguish between people who would like to join in and are not succeeding, and people who are quiet by choice. Remind yourself of the many reasons that might lie behind apparent refusal to speak. First, the more junior people are, the more likely it is that they will feel at least a little intimidated by speaking up in front of seniors. People with a preference for introversion need time to get their thoughts in order and in a group of noisy extraverts, this may seem impossible, or else the point they might have made, if given time, is made by someone else and they do not want to seem as if they are merely repeating an opinion already expressed. People who lack self-confidence may hesitate to join in, dreading looking foolish because they fear their opinions are shallow and self-evident. Others may not know the typical protocols of a facilitated meeting so remain silent as self-protection or possibly may believe that if they do speak their voices are too quiet to be heard. In multinational groups there may be people who are uncertain about their grasp of a language that is not their mother tongue and who therefore hold back.

To deal with the issue of under-contributors, you need to notice them. Make a habit of constantly scanning the room to see who is speaking and who is not. You cannot intervene if you do not know that there is a problem.

All these tactics are worth a try:

- Stating at the outset that some people typically contribute less than others and asking, 'What can we do to ensure that these quieter people get the chance to speak?' It is also helpful to say, 'There will be people here who always have a lot to say. What do those people suggest to ensure that the people who typically say less, get their moments as well?'

- Designing ice-breakers (see p. 71) that ensure everyone has said something at the beginning of the meeting. The longer people go without speaking, the less likely it is that they will speak at all.

- Designing many small group activities where it is easier for more reticent people to participate.

- Making sure that you constantly keep eye contact with the quieter people so that they know you are noticing them. If they do show signs of wanting to speak, this makes it more likely that you will be alert to their signals.

- Inviting people with known expertise to contribute. It is better to do this by general rather than specific invitation; that is, 'Would anyone who knows something about X topic like to say something here?' rather than 'Richard, you're an expert on X, what do you think?'

- Looking in someone's direction and pausing expectantly may prompt them to contribute; so might encouraging them with nods and smiles.

- Encouraging an under-contributor when they do speak by saying 'That sounds interesting – can you stay with that point?' or, 'Could you tell us some more about that?'

- When a discussion appears to be reaching its natural end, reining it in and saying, 'Let's give the people who have had less to say the opportunity to add anything they have observed, want to reinforce or want to add . . .' Then you look in the direction of these people, creating the space for them to speak if they wish. Often this will produce a shrewd additional opinion or confirmation of a decision.

An extreme form of under-contributing is the person who constantly yawns and eventually falls asleep. Discreetly checking later with the person concerned why this happened is probably the best tactic. Do not jump to the conclusion that boredom was the cause. Other explanations might include: illness, having to take medication which induces drowsiness, eating or drinking too much at lunch, hangovers or inability to understand whatever is under debate.

Over-contributors

Assume that at any facilitated event there will be someone who talks too much. The over-talker's reasons may include knowing more than others and wanting to share what they know, being the boss or more senior and having become accustomed to speaking a lot at meetings; seeking recognition from others in the group: wanting prominence; making a bid to control the group: wanting dominance. Others are just habitual over-talkers with little idea of how their obsessive soliloquizing affects others. A peculiarly annoying variant here is the narcissist who relentlessly brings everything back to themselves and at great length.

Like every other issue in facilitation, there is no perfect strategy that will work every time. You might try any of the following:

- Raising the probability at the outset that some people will talk more than others and agreeing a protocol with the group for dealing with it.
- Where semi-formal presentations are involved, agreeing strict time limits and a method of alerting the speaker to the fact that time is running out followed by a way of guillotining a presentation that is going on too long. For instance, I learned a series of hand-signals from floor managers during my TV career and now routinely agree with them in such situations: a whole hand held up in the speaker's eye line to indicate five minutes left, two fingers for two minutes, two crossed fingers for half a minute.

Additional tactics

- Ignoring the bids the person makes to speak, and bringing in someone else instead.
- Interrupting yet another very long speech at a pause for breath by saying something like 'X, I'm aware that Y is trying to get into the conversation; can we come back to you later?'
- Shutting them out with discreet hand or body movements; for instance, the 'traffic cop' signal – a hand held palm-out lightly as an instruction not to speak while also bringing in someone else with your other hand.
- Interrupting courteously and asking the group whether it is helping them to hear so much from one person.

A particularly difficult form of over-contributor is the one who speaks at length on topics that seem irrelevant to the main purpose of the day. First, be clear in your own mind that what they are saying really is irrelevant, especially if you are new to the group and the subject. However, if you get clear signals that X is off again on a favourite hobby horse, then try stopping the person by saying warmly and respectfully, 'X can I stop you there. I'm not really clear how this is relevant to our topic. Can you spell that out to me?' This is usually enough to introduce some self-editing on the over-contributor's part and if done good-naturedly is unlikely to cause offence. Asking it as a question also introduces the possibility that an apparent over-contributor does actually have something important to say.

Some over-contributors simply repeat the same thought many times. If this person is also angry they may distract the group, sucking energy, most of it negative, into unproductive areas. My belief when I encounter this phenomenon is that the person does not feel heard and that they are operating on the simplistic assumption that just going on saying the same thing will eventually batter people into taking notice. In fact, of course, the opposite happens – the group switches them off mentally, thus ensuring that the annoying repetition continues.

When I meet this behaviour, I have a strategy that rarely fails. It can feel counter-intuitive because it appears as if you are actually giving the person yet more airtime when what most people in the group want is for them to shut up. Create the space in the group by stopping the discussion and saying, 'X, I notice you've been making the same point many times this morning. This suggests to me that you believe it is important. Can you summarize for us very briefly what the core of your thinking is here?' A lucid explanation usually follows from X. If it shows signs of being too long, interrupt and ask for a précis in the interests of everyone's time. You then complement the process by *offering your own summary*. Finally, you ask the group for brief responses and run a crisp discussion in the usual way. X then sinks back into the chair, satisfied that at last some proper attention has been paid and rarely returns to the by now tediously familiar point. If, however, this happens, then you can interrupt again, this time challenging X on whether or not a new line of reasoning is going to be put forward.

Both over- and under-contributors can be encouraged to look at the impact of their behaviour through process review (p. 134).

The boss takes over

As the event continues, the boss begins to do more and more of the talking. In fact, it starts to seem like just another example of the meetings that people have already described to you where the hour-long weekly departmental meetings consist of 55 minutes of the boss talking and 5 minutes of fawning questions from his underlings. At your event, other people talk less and less. They begin to glance at their watches ('When can we get away? When will this be over?'). This is an extreme version of the over-talker and it is one that many facilitators find excruciating.

The solution is entirely in the preparation. It is always too late on the day.

What to do

- Confront the possibility openly ahead of the event. Remind the boss that hierarchy is ever present in human groups and that the aim is for them to be participants along with everyone else. Explain the benefit of this: they can relax and enjoy the lack of responsibility for the day; listen as well as talk.
- Help the boss prepare the opening 5–10 minutes (p. 69) and suggest rehearsing it with you.
- Encourage the boss to say constantly during the event that they want people to contribute to the full; promising that they are open to all suggestions and feedback.
- Coach the boss in how to share the facilitation – summarizing and noticing process patterns rather than contributing on the content; putting their ideas as questions rather than statements; holding back from offering solutions too soon.
- Agree a private signal that will alert them to any tendency to say too much.
- Make sure that the day includes plenty of opportunities for people to work in pairs, trios and quartets.
- Give the boss a starring role at the action-phase discussion, but counsel them against taking on all the responsibility for follow-up.

Late arrivals, early departures

This may be a form of acting out, where people display their feelings about the event, the organization or their boss through allegedly urgent matters that delay them or require an early departure. Alternatively, there may be flimsy excuses about traffic on the motorway. In London, the vagaries of the under-ground system can be a popular and convenient fictional cover for lateness. This is a peculiarly disruptive form of protest, if protest it is, and of course it may not be – the explanations may be genuine. Equally, when one person leaves early, assume the event is over to all intents and purposes as everyone else will feel resentful at the interruption and perhaps wish they, too, were leaving. You may see versions of the same behaviour during breaks where people insist on making long calls on their mobiles rather than return-ing on time.

What to do

Again this is best dealt with in advance by asking your client to emphasize the importance of prompt starts and staying for the full event. On the day itself you can negotiate punctuality as part of the ground rules phase (p. 69), making it clear that regardless of whether you have a quorum, you will be starting on time. Where people are tardy in returning after breaks, and punctuality has been agreed as a ground rule, point out the discrepancy and discuss how and why it is happening. Sometimes there may be simple explanations; for instance, long queues for the lavatories or an agonizingly slow coffee dispenser.

Emphasize the importance of staying for the full length of the event and ask whether anyone has to leave early. Explain the impact of early departures on the rest of the group. Feeble excuses are usually flushed out by this process and often the person finds that magically they can sort the problem without leaving before everyone else. If people do arrive late, stop the discussion and wait for the person to find their seat. Do not reward the behaviour by in effect restarting the event or 'explaining' what they have missed but do not glare or frown either.

Be reasonable: genuine crises do happen. I was running an event where we had negotiated rules along these lines. Halfway through, I was timidly approached by one participant to say she had just had a text saying that her daughter had given birth to a premature baby now in intensive care and her daughter was very distressed so she hoped it was all right to leave. Of course it was and I felt later that perhaps I had been over-fierce in my warnings. On 7 July 2005, I was running an event for clinicians at University College Hospital in London. We started promptly at 9 a.m. By 9.45 a.m. I had no one left in the group: all had been bleeped to deal with the aftermath of the terrorist attack on London and I saw many of them again on the news that evening as they treated casualties.

Your authority is directly challenged

Your authority may be challenged in a number of ways. These include the distracting behaviour, late arrivals and early departures discussed above. But you may also experience direct challenges. These may involve abrupt mass refusal to take part in an activity, or they may be verbal and take the form of 'Why are we here?' or 'This is boring' or 'What are they paying you to do this?' or 'We've been talking about this group, and we don't like the way it's going'.

Sometimes a rival facilitator emerges. The challenger begins to suggest alternative ways of running the discussion, or offers a 'better' ice-breaker or a different method for making a decision. You will have to decide whether the purpose is helpfulness, even if presented clumsily, or a direct challenge. I was running an event for the global HR team of a company and was aware that everyone present was also an experienced facilitator. About two hours in, one person began making innumerable alternative suggestions about the design of the day, followed by some further suggestions from her colleagues. Quickly I had to ask myself: 'Was this feedback for me? Were these ideas actually better than my own? Was it a challenge? Should I go along with them out of courtesy and to demonstrate openness?' In this case my on-the-spot conclusion was 'none of the above'. I politely thanked the people who had offered their ideas, acknowledged that any one of the people present could come up with superb ideas for running the day but that was my job and to prevent unproductive discussion about methodology, I suggested that we stick with my plan for the day. Relief all round as the alternative facilitator settled back into her chair. She explained later that her suggestions had merely been offered as 'compulsive helpfulness'.

There is a difference between participants who offer observations on group process (useful) and people who could potentially derail the meeting by seeming to suggest that they always have a better idea about how to run it (not useful).

The most effective tactics to deal with challenges to your authority are:

- Listen carefully, reflecting back and summarizing what the person is saying, showing that you understand their concerns.
- Avoid getting defensive.
- Consider what useful truth there might be in what they are saying and make changes if necessary.
- Ask the group what they would like to see or do instead but keep this brief.
- Check with the rest of the group whether the critical opinion is widely shared. Often this will reveal that it is not and that views divide along fault lines in the group's own dynamics.

A point to note here is that you do not have to take rudeness from a participant. Facilitator neutrality does not include being a punchbag for verbal abuse or being unassertive. This breathtaking example was described to me by a colleague:

> It was a tense moment in the group because we were looking at relationships within it and the discussion had revealed a high level of jealousy, spite and anger. The organisation prided itself on its intellectual sophistication but the idea of emotional intelligence was new to them and this was the focus of the event. One man suddenly

swung round, stared at me and said he resented having a 'working class philistine' like me (I still have my regional accent) running the discussion. The whole room became still and I was aware of everyone's eyes on me. I stayed surprisingly calm, because I guessed that this was more about him than me, took several breaths to steady myself and said, 'X, I find that remark offensive and I think you will want to apologise to me'. He went very red and mumbled something which possibly included the word 'Sorry'.

Special needs?

This crisis often appears out of the blue. You are jogging along apparently happily when a group member indignantly and angrily raises an issue about some discomfort, apparent insult or breach of principle. Where principle is invoked, it can often mean that the stately ideology of equal opportunities is invoked, with an alleged 'victim' of discrimination complaining, making speeches to denounce 'management' and potentially derailing the whole event. Sometimes, there is just an unfortunate clash of needs, as in this example described to me by a colleague:

> I was facilitating a workshop about coaching with 100 people. I was doing a 'live' demonstration of coaching and we had just started when a woman stood up at the front and said that because she was deaf she needed to have adjustments made to the loop system. We paused while this happened. We started again and again she interrupted to say she could not see our faces so could we move off the platform area and on to the floor. So we did. She then said she couldn't see our lips so could we move again. This time I had to say no as there was restiveness in the room and there was a limit to how far you can accommodate one person's needs against so many others' so I politely explained that we could not make any more changes but would be happy to talk her through the process individually afterwards. I did ask if there was anyone in the audience who could sign. There wasn't. I don't blame her – she was interested and wanted to be there, but the sponsoring client should have alerted me and provided the help she needed.

Cure: remember to ask in advance if anyone has special needs. These could include physical mobility as well as sensory problems. If, despite this, you have a problem, then try to accommodate it as quickly and courteously as possible, but sometimes, as above, it is not sensible to delay and disturb 99 people for the sake of finding an elaborate solution for one of them.

Occasionally, participants will claim special needs even though there is nothing obviously different or unusual about them, as in this example from a colleague in higher education:

> Mature students are listening to a panel of academics talk about different research methodologies they had used in their work. In the middle of one professor's talk, a woman stands up and says, 'This isn't meeting my learning needs.' The effect was to halt the lecture and spark a disconnected discussion about learning needs, what the University does or doesn't do to meet them, etc, sidetracking a perfectly good presentation. Eventually another professor left the room with her to provide a one-on-one session where her 'learning needs' could be met.

Figure 6.2
Source: Stephen Appleby (2006b)

This was a poor option in my view, giving undue attention to someone who probably did not need it. A more effective intervention would have been for the Chair to have referred to the agenda and invited the participant to leave, if the event wasn't working for her, inviting her to meet him after the panel discussion to review her objections.

Sometimes the complaint is just unreasonable, as here:

> We were working on a residential course and the hotel was unusually full. I had a suite with a completely separate sitting room. To get

around the problem, we were using this as a break-out room. A woman in the group raised a huge storm about being 'forced to be in a man's bedroom' and said it was an insult to all the women in the group who would feel terrible embarrassment. I think my sense of insult was actually greater than hers. Did she really think there was going to be some kind of mass rape?

What did this facilitator do? He asked the other women if they felt the same. The answer was no. He gave the complainant the chance to change groups, which she did.

This example was sent to me by a US colleague:

A committee was meeting to discuss candidates for a senior job. We had interviewed three candidates, two women and one man. One of the women was African American. It was clear to the majority of us on the committee that the African American candidate didn't have the necessary qualifications or skills for the position. When I suggested that she be eliminated from the short list, one of the committee members, who is also African American, responded, 'You're saying that because you're a member of the dominant culture.' The effect was to halt any real discussion on the professional qualities of the candidates. Group members either went silent or tried to talk around the issue. The effect of this use of the 'race card' was to intimidate other members of the committee.

My colleague comments: If the person chairing the meeting had been more confident, he might have asked her to identify which particular qualities of this applicant the other members of the committee had overlooked – given her space to speak; in other words, but in a directed way.

These challenges are often used by participants as a smokescreen. At one workshop, just as we were about to embark on a 'difficult' exercise, I was challenged by a participant about using flip charts instead of PowerPoint on the grounds that *if* there had been a dyslexic person present (there was not) this hypothetical person *might* hypothetically have had difficulty reading the flip chart. This could easily have degenerated into a long and pointless theoretical debate about accessibility in general and I saw immediately how other participants were readying themselves to leap to my defence. I politely asked the complainant to reserve her comments to the final feedback session of the workshop, reassuring her that I would be interested to hear them along with other feedback.

In general you need to distinguish between a genuine and important breach of principle that might need immediate action, and the posturing or special pleading that will quickly derail your event if not brought to a courteous halt.

Open conflict breaks out

Both you and your group may be alarmed and frightened by conflict, even though finding out how not to run away from conflict may be one of the main lessons the group can learn from its time together. For instance, a dysfunctional work team will, by definition, be unable to deal with conflict. Typically, it will be indulging in corridor politics where pairs or trios say to each other the things they cannot say when the whole group is in session. Or perhaps you will see occasional outbreaks of bitterness and sarcasm where people say tart and hurtful things about each other.

Another version of the same phenomenon is the group where one or two people hold out for their own point of view, despite seeing that everyone else has found a consensus. I remember an awayday for a group that I was managing at the time where the then thorny topic of smoking in the office was under discussion. One of the smokers persisted in maintaining that it was an infringement of her freedom to be asked to give up smoking and also alleged that the claim of one member of the group to be allergic to cigarette smoke was 'rubbish'. It is a hard lesson for many people to learn that living and working in groups does often involve giving up individual freedoms and that having your own way all the time is simply not possible. Equally, it is often useful for facilitators to point out that absolute agreement is not the purpose of a facilitated discussion. The best outcome will be one that everyone feels they can live with – a significantly different emphasis.

What to do

Stay calm and firm. Never become an onlooker: your authority will be destroyed if you do and it is equally ineffectual to plead feebly with the fighters to stop. You must confidently challenge behaviour that is unacceptable especially when it clearly runs counter to the ground rules that have been agreed at the beginning of the event.

Any of these tactics may be worth trying:

- Name it as an impasse or a crisis. *So we've got a conflict here and we need to deal with it before we can go on.*
- Ask people to state their underlying assumptions; for instance, saying, 'When you say that it's footling asking for financial information from John, could you tell us what your assumption is here?'
- Ask what further facts or other information would help.
- Ask the group whether this is something that should be dealt with

inside or outside the event and discussion. For instance, for deep-seated conflicts, formal mediation might be better than attempting to resolve it on the spot.

- Clarify and summarize the issues as both sides see them.
- Identifying the areas of agreement: these are often more extensive than the areas of disagreement, but it is easy to lose sight of this in the heat of the debate.
- Set up reverse role plays where each side swaps roles and describes how they think their behaviour would look to the other.
- 'Fishbowls' where each side observes the other in discussion (see also p. 86)
- Exploring what the outcome is likely to be if there is no resolution.
- Setting up a pilot project for a limited period of time and then agreeing to evaluate it.
- Re-emphazing or recreating ground rules that will help the group deal with conflict.
- Referring the group to theoretical ideas to help them understand their behaviour (i.e. Schutz, p. 43 or Bion, p. 28).

These are just some of the possible strategies. Whatever you do, the most important message will be conveyed by your own behaviour. If you retreat to the sidelines, the group will see your own belief about the danger of conflict. If you stay with it, they will see that you believe in the possibility of solutions.

Just occasionally – possibly only once in any facilitator's career – it may be clear that conflict is so deep-rooted that it is pointless to continue the event. My colleague Phil Hayes describes facilitating such an event for warring surgeons in an English hospital, two of whom had not spoken to each other for several years despite being in the same department and being required to work together. At the second of what had been planned as several day-long team-building events, it was clear to Phil that nothing had changed since the first event. The self-styled 'old bulls' were as aggressive as ever to each other. After the first hour, Phil stopped the discussion, said he felt he and they were at a turning point and announced quietly and firmly that he was going to take a walk around the hospital grounds for 30 minutes, during which time they should decide whether it was worth continuing. His own respectfully stated condition for going on with the programme was their agreement that change was possible, with each person responsible for being able to make changes that would benefit the whole group. When he returned, it was to be told that they had agreed to stop – possibly the first thing on which the whole group had agreed for some years. Phil felt that he had acted with integrity. To have continued in such dire circumstances could only have left both him and the group with deep feelings of failure. As it was, all involved were able to make a considered and dignified decision. This story also shows that such apparent endings and 'failures' are not everything they seem. Three months later, the two most stubbornly stuck members of this group had resigned; one to move on to another job and the other one to retire. My hunch is that Phil's excellent facilitation had exposed the difficulties – and their probable consequences for the team, for patients and other staff – in a way that made it impossible for them to be concealed or tolerated any longer.

Whisperers

You notice that there are outbreaks of pair or trio chatting, laughing, note-passing and whispering. It has become a pattern. It is disruptive. You cannot ignore this behaviour or pretend it is not happening, nor can you resort to high-handed teacher-like behaviour such as demanding haughtily that the offenders 'share the joke'. It is much better to assume that the behaviour is merely a symptom of some other problem and you cannot know what this is until you ask the people concerned. I was running a series of half-day events for an organization that was introducing a new pay structure. At one such event for a department with a newly appointed head, a group of senior people sat at the back and were soon passing each other notes like naughty schoolchildren. I found their behaviour astounding, especially as their boss was present and had only just finished an elegant summary of the new arrangements. What I had foolishly omitted to ask in advance was whether everyone present was a volunteer. It quickly became clear that the answer was 'no'.

What to do

- Stop the general discussion.
- Use feedback principles (see p. 131). Courteously say:

  I notice that in the last 10 minutes or so, X, Y and Z have been having private chats. I'm finding it distracting. You now look around the rest of the group. *'How do others feel?'* You wait for the response.

- The chances are that the rest of the group will speak indignantly and agree with you. Do not join in the disapproval. Instead, say, 'When people do this, it's often because they have some concern that is not being raised with the group. Is that true for you?' Even if this is not the cause, it allows people to state any dissatisfaction they feel. When the cause is stated, discuss it with the whole group. Depending on the outcome, you might try any of these tactics:

- Agree a rule with the group about general behaviour to prevent it happening again.
- Firmly ask the gossipers to keep their chat until the break.
- Split the group into pairs or trios with a topic to discuss and on which to report back.
- As a last resort, be prepared to ask them to leave if they persist.

When I followed the feedback procedure with the group assembled to discuss their new pay deal, I quickly discovered that they had been told it was mandatory to attend and their belief that the new arrangements would disadvantage them. By making it clear that there would be ample time for them to discuss their concerns and also requesting that the whispering should stop, the rest of the session ran to plan. However, their reckless indifference about how their boss perceived such behaviour puzzled me and I made a point of discussing it with her later where she confessed that she had been a surprise choice for her post and felt she had yet to stamp her authority on the group, as was all too evident.

A group member storms out

When this happens it virtually always takes both facilitator and group by surprise. The underlying cause is usually an unresolved conflict between individuals about which you, and possibly the majority of the group, are unaware:

> Although there had been some observable tension in the discussion I was totally amazed when one woman just jumped up out of her seat and ran from the room without saying a word! It was awful because so unexpected.

> It was near the end of a tiring day when one of the most junior people suddenly stood up and announced loudly that she was 'finding this unbearable' and was leaving and swept out of the room before anyone could ask what it was that she was finding 'unbearable'. As it was a residential event for people from all over the globe, no one knew whether 'leaving' meant she was intending to go back to New York or just leaving the room. Two women ran after her and did not come back. The others just looked pole-axed.

Do not assume you know the reason. It could be that something in the discussion has touched on a sensitive subject for the person who rushes out and they do not want others to see the depth of their distress. It could be a planned protest or part of some long-running feud between individuals. Never pretend the walk-out has not happened, for instance, by saying, 'Ah well these things happen. Now, let's see, where were we?' An abrupt departure is a dramatic expression of complaint and participants will usually assume that it is a negative judgement on the whole group. It can leave everyone, including you, feeling any mix of: upset, startled, excited, worried, ashamed, guilty . . . and it is impossible to go on until you have dealt with it. A further complication is that if the person has acted impulsively they may already be feeling they have lost face and dread re-entering the group.

What to do

- Do not run after the person yourself – your duty is with the group.
- Ask if anyone can shed light on the incident. Usually there will be at least one person who can. Their explanation may quickly degenerate into gossip. If it does, stop it and discourage any negative comment on the absentee.
- Ask how the group feels, for instance, by saying, 'People usually find it disturbing when something like this happens. How do you feel, now this minute?' Tell the group about your own feelings, though not at length.
- Ask what suggestions the group has about getting the person back in the room and follow up whatever emerges as the consensus.
- Ask how the group would like to deal with the situation; for instance, they might want to take a break or might prefer to carry on. Carrying on is usually a better option
- Seek out the leaver yourself at the next break and ask them what triggered their departure. If it was something you are alleged to have done yourself, express concern at their distress without necessarily apologizing, as you may have nothing to apologize for. If you do have reason to apologize, do so immediately, straightforwardly, briefly and calmly, repeating your apology to the group later.
- Ask what will need to happen for the leaver to return to the group. This could be anything from a few moments to cool off to a formal apology from some other person in the room whom they feel has insulted them.
- Do not over-persuade – there are circumstances where it might be better for the person to leave permanently. If so, check that they are composed enough to be able to make sensible arrangements. If they are still flustered and upset, ask what help they need to organize their departure.

- If and when they do return, welcome them back without fuss but do briefly discuss with the group what needs to be in place to prevent such an incident happening again.

Mobile mobsters

You are deep into the very heart of the discussion when the irritating buzz of the Minute Waltz, the tinny tones of the latest pop craze, or whatever, intrudes. The owner cannot resist answering and either rushes out of the room or answers on the spot. Or, you are doing small group work when a mobile goes off inside someone's bag. The owner is not in the room so which bag is it? The whole group joins in the hunt. And when you have found it, should you pick it up and answer it?

Prevention is better than cure. Remind the group after every break to check that their mobiles are switched off because most people will have used the break to check for messages and it is easy to forget to turn the phone off. At the beginning of the day, ask whether anyone needs to keep theirs on and if so what they will do if it rings. Suggest they have it on vibrate rather than a ring tone. Make sure you check your own.

If a phone does ring, never ignore it. Stop the discussion while the owner fumbles and ask, 'Do you need to answer?' If the response is yes, then encourage them to make a measured exit then check that everyone else has their phones switched off – and check your own.

Tears

You must expect strong emotion in the group. The more important the subject is to its members, the more likely this is. It is inevitable that from time to time someone will become upset and will cry. The keys to how to cope are:

- staying respectful of the other person's dignity
- remaining unruffled yourself
- giving the person the option of stopping or retiring if they wish
- consulting the group about what they would like to do

Here is an example from a senior manager who bravely faced this possibility head on:

I was asked by a team I managed at the time to run a day where the topic was stress. Many of the team had significant crises in their personal lives and the organisation was also changing in ways that they found uncomfortable. The hazard here was of creating an over-heated atmosphere. I began the workshop by drawing attention to this danger and by encouraging people to enter the discussion at whatever levels felt comfortable for them. Perhaps half the group did cry as they were describing their feelings. The atmosphere was quiet and supportive. The group also explored what we could do to help each other. Throughout the morning, I constantly checked how we were doing and what the level of comfort was with the atmosphere. People later said the day was a real breakthrough – 'the first time we were really honest with each other'.

It is a mistake to assume that people regret crying and would rather not do it in public or that it is better if people do not cry, or that if you see tears, they should be tactfully ignored. Any of this could be true, depending on the circumstances. But we all make the decision individually about whether or not to expose our emotions in public – in truth it is impossible to be forced to cry – or not to cry.

Conclusion

My experience is that the urge to cover up social embarrassment does not serve facilitators well. It is usually worth surfacing the problem, whatever it is. Trust your instinct that something is wrong. Assume that others in the group are feeling the same. Assume, too, that most people are looking for a positive outcome and will be on your side unless you make a major error. Even if you do make a mistake, ask for the group's help in putting it right, but stay focused and calm. Applying these principles will work 99 per cent of the time.

7   Wrapping it all up

The more I practise, the luckier I get.

(Gary Player, golfer)

Evaluating

When you are coming towards the end of an event, there can be tiredness because of the intensity of the concentration, and a sense of relief that it will soon be over. You and the group can relax, everyone is thinking about what they have to do that evening, or about getting back to their email, or are wondering what the traffic will be like on the way home. Resist the temptation to bring things to a rushed close and in your planning for the day, factor in enough time for evaluation. Every meeting costs time and money, so it matters whether or not it has provided value. Also, there will be a range of views in the group and it is helpful for people to see that sometimes their own firmly held opinions about how brilliant or hopeless the day has been are not necessarily shared by everyone. Remember that you are not looking for consensus; people are not required to vote or pass a resolution, so be prepared to leave things loose in the discussion.

The time you need will depend on purpose and style of the event. A short meeting might be evaluated in five minutes; a one-day awayday might need at least fifteen minutes. Review it from three angles:

1   How far has the event met the task objectives you and the group agreed at the outset?
2   How has it been for the group at the process level?
3   What feedback does the group have for you?

Has the event met its objectives?

Cynicism about facilitated events can sometimes be traced back to simple failure to review whether the day has worked at the task level. 'All we did was sit around having a natter and eating nice food. It cost a bomb and didn't achieve anything'. If you wrote the objectives for the day on a flip chart, return to them now. Take each objective in turn and ask the group how far it has been achieved. It is often the case that, as the event goes on, it becomes clear that an original objective is not achievable within the available resources because discussion has usefully revealed that the problem is too complex. If so, then you will probably have included an action-planning session where the group will have decided how it wishes to pursue the matter.

How has it been for the group at the process level?

The hidden or overt agenda for many meetings is to improve relationships. Often the meeting will be deemed a success if people have been able to speak more personally and directly to each other than they have managed previously. Sometimes it is not so pleasant. Covert conflicts come to the surface and this can be painful or uncomfortable for participants. Some people may feel that there are things that might have been better left unsaid. Others may feel relief that the air has been cleared. Either way, you need to make it possible for people to talk honestly. Some ways of asking questions (see also Process Review, Chapter 5, p. 134) that will reveal how people feel about the emotional content of the event are:

> *How has this event been as an experience?*
>
> *How do you feel now about the state of relationships in the group?*
>
> *What has changed at the emotional level?*
>
> *What will be different in this group as a result of today?*

Feedback for you

Some facilitators aspire to a style of lofty detachment that implies they are so far outside the group that they can be assumed to have suspended all the normal human feelings of vulnerability, the wish to be liked or anxiety about competence. They therefore make it highly unlikely that people will feel able to give them any feedback. Be assured that this kind of facilitator is still the subject of discussion among the group but not to their face.

It is essential to get feedback on how you have run the event. Without feedback you cannot improve. Willingness to ask for feedback, and to receive it without defensiveness also models the kind of behaviour you will probably be advocating for participants. This is especially true if part of the day that you have run has included activities where people have been required to give honest feedback to each other. The more you have run the event in a way that makes it possible for people to speak candidly but respectfully, the easier it will be for people to give you feedback in turn.

All conscientious facilitators ask frequently for feedback during the event, but often this will be most appropriately addressed informally to individuals during breaks. The importance of asking for it in public at the end of the event is that it shows a proper professional concern for improvement and for valuing participants' views.

Questions might include:

> *I'd like to have your feedback on how I've run this event. Could we start with what has gone well from your point of view?*
>
> *What would you have liked me to do differently?*
>
> *If I were running this day again, what advice would you give me about how to make it more effective?*

If participants describe discomfort with the emotional content of the day, they may be inclined to blame you: it was your fault for encouraging people to say or do things that they now regret. When this happens you have to be careful not to accept such blame inappropriately. It could be true that you have been less skilful than is ideal in how you handled the activity or the discussion but it is usually tricky to establish exactly what might have constituted 'skilful' or 'ideal'. Listen to the feedback carefully and neutrally because there may be much to learn from people's comments, even when they are made clumsily or rudely. Clarify, summarize and resist the temptation to be defensive or tart in your response. Bear in mind the principle of choice here: no one can *make* another person happy or unhappy. We are all responsible for our reactions to whatever the stimulus is and at some level, whether awarely or not, we make the choice. When facing painful emotional realities it is sometimes easier for participants to slip into victim mode (see also p. 35) and to try to make someone else responsible for their happiness, which in this case is the facilitator. The same can be true for you: when we hear critical comments there is a temptation to blame the people who made them.

Mostly people's instinct is to be generous or non-committal when asked by a facilitator for feedback. Use your questioning skills to probe appropriately for more detail. 'What specifically did you like/not like about the way I did X or Y?' Clarify comments if necessary and check out how far others in the group agree. It is important not to overdo this phase by letting it take too long or allowing it to get too heavy. Thank people straightforwardly for their feedback and pass on to the closing of the event.

If you prefer alternatives to discussion techniques, here are some further ideas.

Feedback 'gallery'

This works well for a group that is going to meet again; for instance, a learning set or a team that is involved in a series of events.

Everyone writes down everyone's name on a separate flip chart sheet. When everyone has walked around the room quietly and looked at all the comments, have a brief discussion about changes you might make next time you meet (see Table 7.1).

Giving the session a mark

Prepare a flip chart in advance. Divide it into two columns, heading one 'Enjoyable' and the other 'Useful'. On the left-hand side of each column list the numbers 10–1, starting with 10 at the top.

Distribute two identical Post-it notes to everyone. Ask them to head one 'Useful', the other 'Enjoyable'. Ask people, anonymously, to mark the event out of 10 in each category; 10 for excellent, 1 for poor. Gather in the Post-its and quickly record the results on a flip chart (see Figure 7.1).

Explore all the obvious patterns of instance differences between the ratings people give to enjoyable compared with useful. Where people give high marks ask:

- What needs to happen to ensure that the next meeting is as good as this one?
- Where there are low marks, ask people to identify themselves and then say: 'What would need to change to transform the low marks into high ones?'

	Helped us by	Might consider doing differently
Anne		
Stephen		
Geeta		
Warren		
Myself		
Facilitator's name		

Table 7.1

Enjoyable		Useful
✓	10	
✓✓✓	9	✓✓✓
✓	8	
	7	✓✓
	6	
✓	5	
	4	
	3	✓
	2	
	1	

Figure 7.1

Usually, the answers will concern other people hogging the time, or too much of the agenda being devoted to issues seen by them as not being of real importance. Listen carefully to their views and then ask:

- What prevented you raising that issue during the day?
- How could another session be different?

If you are a manager, note that this simple protocol takes only a few moments to do and administering it routinely at the end of every meeting soon raises the quality of the meetings as the people who are inclined to sulk and give low marks all round know that they will be asked why they did not raise their concerns earlier.

Using feedback forms

Sometimes there is a case for asking people to consider their views on paper first. You will get a more thoughtful and in-depth response this way. Explain that writing down comments is a preparatory stage. No one will see what they have written but they will be invited to discuss it.

There are many possible ways this kind of form can be designed. Here is example of a feedback form on a session.

Feedback on today

Please spend a few moments jotting down answers to these questions. No-one else will see your comments, but you will be asked to discuss them.

How far do you feel that today's objectives were:

1   Worth while?

2   Met?

3   How do you feel about your own contribution to the group? Have you been able to say as much and participate as much as you wished? What might have made it a better experience for you?

4   How do you feel about the way the group has performed today? What were the high spots for you? What might have made it a better day from that point of view?

5   How would you rate the facilitator? What do you see as his/her strengths? What could he/she have done to make it a more satisfying experience?

6   What has changed for you today?

Give people about five minutes to complete the form and then run a discussion, taking each point in turn.

The 'teabag technique'

An alternative is to use the form sometimes described as the 'teabag technique'. This is because 'the flavour just floods out'. The open-ended questions encourage a wide range of responses and include the possibility of voicing criticisms of the facilitator.

Here is another example of a feedback form on a session.

Feedback on today

Confidential
Please fill in the form, giving your comments as you see fit.

I've understood

I've learned

I'm surprised

I enjoyed

I'm puzzled

I'm disappointed

I can develop

Any other comments?

Please add your name if you wish

Reviewing the day later

A week or so after the event, a quick informal review with your client if you are a full-time facilitator or with your group if you are a manager or Chair will have two purposes: (1) to ask what has changed as a result of the event, and (2) to ask for considered feedback for you. Questions could include:

- What's the buzz/'word on the street' about our event?
- How do you feel about it yourself now that you're back in the office?
- How are people getting on with the action list that was agreed?
- What feedback (or further feedback) do you have for me about how I ran the day?

Some questions about evaluation

Evaluation is not quite as simple as it may look. How do you really, truly, judge whether an event has been 'successful'? Is it successful if people praise your unique skills? If you feel the warm glow of a job well done? If all the stated objectives have been met? If the participants go home tired but happy? You could answer yes to all these questions and yet the event may not have been successful. For instance see Table 7.2.

In training and development circles there is a useful framework taken from Donald Kirkpatrick's work (1996) that suggests four levels of evaluation. Level 1 is how people feel about the event itself. This will include their views on the venue as well as on your performance and on the substance of the day. Level 2 is about personal learning: what has changed for individuals as a result of attending? Level 3 is about how the learning is being applied and Level 4 is about bottom-line change for the organization. This model shows how tricky it is to do robust evaluation beyond Level 1. It is easy to gather valid views about the event on the day but it becomes harder and harder the more you

People praise your skills	*But they don't know what better facilitation might look like*
You feel satisfied with your own performance	*But the participants may have been skilfully concealing their dissatisfaction under a cloak of politeness; or else possibly you are just self-deluded*
You met all the stated objectives	*But there is no longer-term benefit because you were on the wrong agenda*
The participants are happy	*But their happiness does not necessarily correlate with a successful event*

Table 7.2

progress to Level 4. This is because so many other factors come into play the further away you get from the event itself. For instance, there may have been a restructuring, a new boss, new regulations introduced; in fact, there are so many variables that it is impossible to attribute change to any one event or series of interventions. Other problems about evaluation are that it is usually challenging to agree what would constitute 'success': what criteria would you use? It also matters who does it: an apparently external and 'objective' evaluator may be in practice no more impersonal and fair than an internal person with their own seemingly biased opinions. Just because people have enjoyed an event, this does not guarantee that anything will change; equally, people can dislike an event but positive change may still result from it, sometimes a long time after the event itself. The real nub, however, of what makes evaluation difficult is that it is usually easier to measure tangibles than intangibles and it may be that the intangibles are the really important factors. For instance, you can readily say what the financial investment per person was, but how do you measure any personal growth that individuals might have achieved?

Just because evaluation is complex does not spare us from the attempt to gather feedback, but we must put all feedback into a cautious context before being too swayed by it one way or the other.

Self-development

Facilitator questionnaire

Continuing your own development is a never completed task for any facilitator. Some basic aptitude helps, but most facilitators are made, not born. Rather like learning how to give a presentation, facilitation skill can improve dramatically with practice and feedback.

This questionnaire asks you to rate yourself on a number of areas correlated with successful performance as a facilitator. Fill it in reasonably quickly, ticking the box that represents how you usually behave.

	1	2	DK
Planning: develops specific, achievable but stretching objectives with event sponsors and participants			
Approachability: informal, friendly manner; easy for participants to approach; encourages participants to challenge him or her			
Clarity: explains complex principles and processes in a way that makes them understandable without compromising on the integrity of the ideas; avoids unhelpful jargon			

Courage: stands up for what he or she believes to be right; does not submit to group or individual pressure on important matters

Creativity: finds innovative and interesting ways of running the event

Encouraging risk: creates an environment that encourages people to take risks safely, pushing their own personal boundaries in order to achieve greater learning

Enjoyment: makes the group process enjoyable with a strong element of fun; doesn't take himself or herself too seriously

Participation: manages the group in a way that ensures there is a high level of participation; finds tactful ways of controlling those who over-contribute and encouraging those who under-contribute

Flexibility: able to adapt and see what is critical; changes plans and functions effectively within changing circumstances

Individual consideration: demonstrates that he or she truly cares for each individual; sensitive to individual needs; treats people with dignity and respect; gives those who need it a lot of help

Integrity: makes own ethics and values clear; practises what he or she preaches

Questioning: uses a range of questioning techniques to clarify and draw out meaning

Summarizing: summarizes appropriately in order to give a sense of structure to the discussion

Challenging: presents ideas that oblige participants to question ideas they have never questioned before

Listening: listens carefully and respectfully to what participants have to say and shows that he or she is listening

Managing conflict: handles conflict in the group in a way that ensures the conflict is worked on appropriately

Resilience: remains calm and objective in the face of stressful circumstances; can pace self during an event

Seeking feedback: constantly seeks and learns from feedback on own performance as a facilitator

	1	2	DK
Self-presentation: behaves with naturalness, confidence and composure; addresses a group in a way that makes everyone feel included; has body mannerisms under control			
Structuring learning: structures content in a way that makes it more likely that participants will be able to understand, remember and use it			
Event design: develops and delivers events that are appropriately varied in the methods and pace they employ			
Voice skills: speaks clearly and audibly with well-modulated tone; has verbal mannerisms under control			
Working with co-facilitators: keenly aware of the impact of own behaviour on others; shows sensitivity to the needs and concerns of colleagues; able to learn from and build rapport with colleagues			

Note: 1 = area of strength/feel comfortable about this. 2 = should probably do this more. DK = don't know/not relevant

Thinking now about the most recent event you facilitated:

- How far did the group feel it achieved its objectives?
- How far did you feel you achieved your objectives?
- What range of facilitator styles did you use?
- What did you learn from this event?
- What development needs does it reveal that you have?
- How will you set about meeting these needs?

The form may also be copied and given to colleagues and participants to fill in and then returned to you. If you do this, you will get pricelessly constructive feedback – a range of views on your skills and how you come across to others.

Feedback from colleagues

When you work with another facilitator you have a wonderful opportunity for learning. Do not waste it. Most of the really valuable feedback that I have had as a facilitator has come from this source. Compared with participants, fellow facilitators have permission to be more ruthless, more detailed and also more affirming about the many occasions when you have, for instance, unobtrusively steered a discussion in the right direction. This is because we usually have a clearer idea than participants of the skills involved and a more finely tuned sense of what the alternatives might have been.

Looking after yourself

At the time, all the various jobs I have done in my career have felt taxing. So I have been a teacher in a further education college, an internal adviser to the BBC on education, a TV producer, a commissioning editor, a manager, management consultant, director of a small business and a coach and, while doing all these jobs, would many times come home feeling drained. For sheer terror, there has been nothing to compare with being a TV studio director; for the physical energy required, nothing to beat teaching 16-year-olds who did not want to be there and for the mental concentration involved in intensive listening, nothing more demanding than being a coach.

However, for potential to feel utterly weary at the end of the day, facilitating has to take the prize for me. You need constant watchfulness; you cannot relax for a moment while you are with the group. Breaks for the participants are rarely so for the facilitator because you are on duty the whole time, whether you are formally facilitating or not. You have to project a steady face, you need a high degree of attentiveness, the ability to process data quickly and considerable emotional resilience. No wonder, then, that returning from an assignment where we regularly spent two long days facilitating events for a lively and demanding team, my co-facilitator's first question as we got to the airport lounge would be, 'How many units of alcohol would you like?' Another consultant colleague describes his psychological state after a day of such work as 'post-event psychosis' and claims that he is unable to speak coherently for at least 24 hours afterwards.

Feeling like this may be inevitable, depending on how experienced you are and on your temperament, but be prepared to pace and to take positive steps to look after yourself when you are doing this work. Always try to take a brief break from the group during a lunch hour, even if it is only 10 minutes; do not overeat, even if the participants do, but do not skip meals either, and do control your intake of caffeine. Even if the participants overindulge in alcohol (not at all uncommon for people who may see the day as a rare chance to unwind together) do not do the same.

Prepare for a facilitation session steadily with ample time devoted to design and planning and then at least 10 minutes of quiet thinking time before participants arrive where you consider what the participants will need from you during the day. If you are nervous, learn and then practise the essentials of controlled breathing. Using the techniques of visualizing success is also an excellent way to programme yourself for a positive outcome. Other suggestions from experienced facilitators include these:

- Get some fresh air, whatever the weather, at some point during the day, preferably at every break.
- Get some exercise, even if it is only a brisk 5-minute walk up the road, but 30 minutes of heart-rate-raising activity is even better.
- Do not use every break catching up with your phone calls – it will make you feel harassed and will break your concentration. It also creates the wrong impression with participants as it will look as if your real attention is somewhere else, which it may well be.
- Learn some simple yoga exercises and spend 10 minutes or more doing them.
- For residential events, get to bed early, bring some simple comfort reading with you and unwind with that or watch some undemanding TV; phone home – this will remind you of where your priorities lie.

The facilitator's tightrope

Your own best instrument: yourself

As a facilitator you are your own best instrument. The more you know about yourself and the triggers that could potentially destabilize you, the more effective you are likely to be. For instance, the transactional analysis (TA) perspective (p. 34) applies to you as much as it does to the group. Ask yourself in which ego states you tend to feel most comfortable. Are there some that as a facilitator you overuse, and some that you underuse? Are you tempted to rely too much on Controlling Parent, making too little use of Natural Child? Are you perhaps spending a lot of time as a facilitator in adult state, so that groups see you as perpetually composed and relaxed, but never showing the warmth of Nurturing Parent? There are no right or wrong answers here – just the need to be self-aware and to work on the raw material of your own personality. Perhaps you are attracted by the dependency that the group begins to show. Do you like the idea that the group cannot have a meeting without you? Maybe you feel indignant if you hear that they are going to self-facilitate. There is also a special danger for facilitators in the rescuer role of the Drama Triangle (see page 36). Perhaps you personally abhor conflict and at the events themselves you want everything to be love and peace, but remember that this is your issue. Some conflict is essential – it provides energy for change. If you see a conflict developing beware of believing that it is your role to smooth it all over or of colluding with the apparent victims. Remember, it is their fight, not yours, and if you start rescuing, your fate is likely to be the fate of all rescuers – the rescued turn on you because you have failed to rescue effectively enough.

Psychometric instruments such as the Myers-Briggs Type Indicator (MBTI)™ and the FIRO-B™ are useful short cuts with groups. They provide a safe vocabulary for understanding difference. But your own preferences and needs are just as important because they raise questions like:

- What's my attitude to Inclusion? Do I want to be so far inside this group that I can't facilitate it effectively? Or do I want to be so far outside it that I'm too detached?
- How much influence do I want in this group? Do I need people to share my beliefs in order to feel I'm doing a good job?
- Do I need to feel this group likes me? How much can I tolerate or welcome coolness or warmth from them?
- Do I tend to get fixed on detail and practicality? Am I only interested in ideas and the bigger picture?
- Am I more comfortable with detached 'truths' and theories than with people's feelings? Am I overconcerned with harmony?
- Is my natural tendency to push things to conclusions, or is it to keep things open?

Whatever your own answers to these questions, remember that others may see them entirely differently, so you are unlikely to be able to meet everyone's needs perfectly.

There are several points to make about the different facilitator styles and techniques:

- You need to be able to use all of them.
- Some are higher risk than others and need a higher degree of skill, confidence and practice.
- All of us tend to overuse one or two styles.
- It is possible to use a style well or badly.
- Being aware of which styles you underuse or overuse is an essential prelude to learning how to extend your range as a facilitator.
- When you know you need more practice in one area, ask an experienced colleague to sit in and observe you in order to give you feedback.

Managing the ambiguities

Expertly good facilitation is hard to pin down: the more you peer at it, the more it seems to vanish. I have come to appreciate that facilitation is a constant balancing act between undesirable extremes, and yet there will be times when even the extremes are justified by the circumstances. So facilitation is always about managing the ambiguities and making the best decision you can, given the circumstances and people on the day.

Control – or standing back?

When you begin to work as a facilitator, your main concern may be to feel in control throughout the event. This is understandable given how frightening it can feel when you are faced with a group apparently depending on you to give the event shape and direction. Yet if you act on the belief that you must be in control the whole time, you will soon have an unsatisfactory event. The participants need to share the control with you: if this does not happen they will soon start behaving in a childlike way; either submitting passively, or rebelling and challenging. Yet here is the heart of the dilemma. If you abandon control, that may not be satisfactory either. When training new facilitators, I have often noticed that the typical temptations seem to be polarized: to intervene too much or not to intervene at all. If facilitators adopt the approach of doing too much, they dominate. If there is too little intervention then the discussion eddies around the hapless facilitator who is soon ignored by everyone.

Skilled facilitation is about knowing when it is vital to be in control and when to step back and this is always a matter of finely balanced judgement on the day – there is no one right answer.

Solutions and closure – or living with chaos?

Facilitated events are usually about exploring problems of one kind or another. There may be a new group who need to get to know one another better, there may be tension between customers and suppliers that needs to be explored, there may be issues of workload, performance or role. The group will be hoping to find a solution to whatever the problems are but it is not your role to find the solution. Your role is to help the group by creating the frameworks that will make finding a solution more likely. However, if you take too laid-back an approach and do not press the group at the appropriate points, then it may be unlikely that it will find the solutions it so urgently needs.

Big issues or bite-sized chunks?

There is an art in the design and preparation of the event that brings this particular ambiguity to the surface. Organizations are often faced with huge issues – a major restructuring, a new system that will change every aspect of the way the group is to work and so on. If your event focuses on issues that are so big that the group cannot hope to influence them, then it is highly likely that feelings of helplessness will be the result. If you encourage the group to focus down on the micro issues, then you risk it responding by telling you that these issues are too small to matter and why are we spending our time discussing trivia?

Being wise or knowing nothing?

The group may expect you to have some ideas to dispense about their issues. However, if you behave as if you are the only source of wisdom, you will soon infantilize them and will also draw inevitable attacks on the actual intelligence and helpfulness of your remarks. On the other hand, if you appear to have nothing to offer, the group may be disappointed. Part of the facilitator role is to help the group create meaning out of their experience. When appropriate, it is often helpful to offer stories – carefully edited to remove identifying details – parallels, ideas and theories that have a bearing on the issues at hand. If you overdo it, you will look self-indulgent. On the other hand, if you do not do it at all and appear to be a blank sheet, you may be denying the group ideas from which they could learn.

Self-aware or self-obsessed?

Most beginner-facilitators are agonizingly self-conscious. It is hard to get away from feeling mercilessly exposed with all those eyes in the room on you. To facilitate well, you need to be highly self-aware. You need to know your own prejudices, biases and hot buttons. You need to recognize when something touches a part of you that you may prefer to keep hidden. However, as a facilitator, you also need to be able to forget yourself and concentrate on the group. As long as you are only thinking about yourself, you will be unable to give anything of any value to the group.

It may be particularly worth thinking about this issue when you are in the middle of painful times in your own life. More than a decade ago, Charlotte, my 22-year-old god-daughter whom I dearly loved, lay dying, the result of a sudden and catastrophic illness, in the intensive care unit of a London hospital. For the month that she was there, I carried on with some of my normal work, including doing some facilitating for the board of an NHS Trust. I knew that my main client also had some serious difficulties in her personal life – her adult daughter had a grave mental illness and was in crisis. Our joint solution here was to discuss it openly. We also agreed to tell the group that we would both need some private time during the lunch break and why, without making an overdramatic emotional statement. I was aware during that day of being on autopilot, but also aware that I could still function well enough. Bringing the issue into the open had some interesting effects. During the day, three members of a team of eight people quietly told me of crises in their own lives – a wife with cancer, a distressing career dilemma and the problems of living with a disabled child. So out of nine of us in the room, five of us had some serious issues in our private lives. I have come to see that this was not in any way extraordinary. When you look just a little below the surface of seemingly tranquil lives, this is what you uncover.

While it is obviously important to behave in a professional way, I believe it is wrong to think that you always have to maintain a cool professional façade when you are facilitating. 'Professional' does not mean that you never show emotion. This is pseudo-professionalism and groups see through it straight away. You have to be authentic, disclosing something of yourself when appropriate. You can be judiciously open about your fallibilities and mistakes – paradoxically, that will make you more acceptable as a competent facilitator. However, it is possible to get this wrong. I worked on one project in the USA involving consulting skills as part of a faculty that included a distinguished US professor. Our participants were a sullen and only-reluctantly-there collection of senior partners from a global accountancy firm, now defunct. The professor made what to me was a wryly self-deprecatory and amusing presentation to the group involving many of his own early errors. The purpose was to show how even someone of his eminence could get it wrong. Many in the group entirely missed the subtlety and real intention of this noble aim. Their response was, 'Why is this guy teaching us if he's made so many mistakes?'

Being liked or being challenging?

We all need to be liked, but the group may not always be the best forum for this need to be met. Of course it is more pleasant if the group likes you, but if this gets in the way of your ability and willingness to challenge them, then you have reached dangerous territory. Being 'nice' may start to take up far too much of your time and energy and you will also come across as insincere and gushing when one of your main tasks as a facilitator is to remain authentic. On the other hand, if all you do is challenge, then you may provoke the kind of deep hostility from the group that makes your work with them impossible.

In such cases I stay with my belief that clients are paying me to tell them the truth as I see it but that it is not my job to be destructive, and I have to be careful not to exaggerate. It is my job to distinguish between fact and interpretation, between description and evaluation. It is also my job to support such clients generously as they struggle with their own feelings of incompetence or despair when the discussion reveals a less optimistic picture than they have expected. Sometimes you may feel you have to press on rather than give way before the client's apparent fragility.

Occasionally, this may be too much for the client. The client associates you with the gloomy message you have brought, or that your facilitation with the group has revealed. In such cases, your association with the client may come to an abrupt end. That could be hard. You may feel personally disliked; indeed, you could be personally disliked and therefore feel hurt and wounded by the unfairness of it all. If this happens, remind yourself that you do not need all clients everywhere and at all times to like you. It is more agreeable if they do, but it is more important to do your job as well as you can while remaining sensitive to how others are perceiving you.

Keeping things calm or stirring up emotion?

The dilemma here is about judging your moment. As a facilitator you may need at various times to act at both ends of this spectrum, but it all depends on the situation and the people. As with so many of the other subtle issues in facilitation, the starting point is self-knowledge. If you are overconcerned about keeping things calm, then look to yourself – what does this fear of anger and emotion tell you? If your temptation is to want the group to be in emotional turmoil, then what need does this liking for drama – and possibly for power – fulfil for you? Be wary of any facilitator who tells you that there must be catharsis or that there must be tranquillity. Both these approaches lead to bogus events. For a start, with artificial catharsis, participants may start playing the personal confession game. This may end up being a little like certain kinds of religious occasion where people are expected to confess to sins that they may or may not have committed and about which they may or may not feel guilty. Participants resort, in other words, to pseudo-disclosure. These approaches leave participants feeling manipulated and ashamed. They give facilitation a bad name.

At the same time, it is often necessary and right that conflicts should be laid open. The feeling that 'we had a meeting/awayday but nothing's really changed' can often be traced back to the joint collusion of group and facilitator in tacitly refusing to get below the logic of the issues in order to look at the emotions. Our apparent rationality and concern with task is only a veneer. If things are to change, then the emotions need to be exposed.

Personal charisma or personal invisibility?

As a facilitator, you must have personal presence. You need to be able to create an impression of reliability, steadiness and authority. But like most kinds of leadership, this authority is most effective when it is lightly worn. There will be times when you need to be vivid. You will always need to be able to gain people's attention readily. Yet there will also be times when you will be most effective if you are seemingly saying and doing nothing.

Be a strong presence	Yet	don't dominate
Provide frameworks	Yet	don't close things down too soon
Focus on the big issues	Yet	keep the issues within manageable bounds
Observe carefully	Yet	don't over-interpret
Create a pleasant atmosphere	Yet	be capable of living with tension and difficulty in the group
Be tough and able to confront	Yet	avoid being hurtful
Be supportive	Yet	don't try to be a buddy
Show interest in others	Yet	look out for fostering dependency
Express your feelings	Yet	don't burden the group with your problems
Be patient, keep things open	Yet	provide structure and closure when necessary
Invite feedback on your work	Yet	stay clear in your own mind about whether criticism is deserved or not
Stay in the present – the here and now	Yet	make links with the past and future
Work with the group's issues	Yet	be prepared to offer your own ideas and experiences when appropriate
Work from a posture of 'creative indifference'	Yet	convey intense interest in the subject being discussed

Table 7.3

This can be a hard balance to achieve. You need to be credible to groups, yet achieve this without undue boasting about your previous triumphs. You need to attract members of the group into wanting to talk to you and spend time with you, yet this is not about being seductive nor about creating dependency. You cannot be a buddy to group members – your value is in being separate. You need to be able to talk about your own values without conveying that you think this is the one right way to be. You need to be an authoritative presence, yet be able to fit in with others from a wide range of temperaments and professions. You need to be available to others and allow them to get to know you better without making unnecessarily intimate revelations.

Summary

One way of looking at facilitation is to see it as a perpetual balancing act between extremes.

These are tough balances to achieve. If you overuse a strength, it can be as destructive as underusing a particular skill. After many years of working as a facilitator, I have come to believe that these ambiguities are not a simple set of either/or options. Often what is required is the both/and approach. For instance, as a facilitator, you need to be both self-aware and other-aware; both charismatic and invisible, both supportive and challenging, and so on. With training and experience you will begin to trust your judgement that these subtleties are possible. Of course there will be times when you will get it wrong, but these are also times for learning and reflection and for understanding that becoming an effective facilitator is a lifetime's work.

Bibliography

Appleby, S. (2006a) Yawn, in L. Graessle, G. Gawlinski and M. Farrel (eds) *Meeting Together*. London: Planning Together.

Appleby, S. (2006b) Me, me, me, in L. Graessle, G. Gawlinski and M. Farrel (eds) *Meeting Together*. London: Planning Together.

Appleby, S. (2006c) I'm a vegetarian, in L. Graessle, G. Gawlinski and M. Farrel (eds) *Meeting Together*. London: Planning Together.

Argyris, C. (1990) *Overcoming Organizational Defenses*. Boston, MA: Allyn & Bacon.

Asch, S.E. (1951) Effects of group pressure on the modification and distortion of judgements, in H. Guetzkow (ed.) *Groups, Leadership and Men*. Pittsburgh: Carnegie Press.

Belbin, R.M. (2004) *Management Teams: Why they Succeed or Fail*, 2nd edn. Oxford: Elsevier Butterworth-Heinemann.

*Bens, I. (2005) *Advanced Facilitation Strategies*. San Francisco, CA: Jossey-Bass.

Berne, E. (1968) *Games People Play*. Middlesex: Penguin.

Bion, W.R. (1961) *Experiences in Groups*. London: Tavistock Publications.

Block, P. (1981) *Flawless Consulting*. San Diego, CA: Pfieffer.

*Bunker, B.B. and Alban, B.T. (1996) *Large Group Interventions: Engaging the Whole System for Rapid Change*. San Francisco, CA: Jossey-Bass.

Casey, D. ([1993] 1996) *Managing Learning in Organizations*. Milton Keynes: Open University Press.

Cockman, P., Evans, B. and Reynolds, P. (1999) *Consulting for Real People*, 2nd edn. Maidenhead: McGraw-Hill.

Cooperrider, D. and Whitney, D. (2005) *Appreciative Inquiry: A Positive Revolution in Change*. San Francisco, CA: Berrett-Koehler.

De Bono, E. (1989) *Six Thinking Hats*. London: Viking.

Fisher, R. and Ury, W. (1981) *Getting to Yes*. New York: Penguin.

*Ghais, S. (2005) *Extreme Facilitation*. San Francisco, CA: Jossey-Bass.

Golding, W. (1954) *Lord of the Flies*. New York: Berkley Publishing Group.

*Graessle, L., Gawlinski, G. and Farrel, M. (2006) *Meeting Together*. London: Planning Together.

Harvey, J. (1988) *The Abilene Paradox and other Mediations on Management*. Lexington, MA: Lexington Books.

Hawkins, P. and Smith, N. (2006) *Coaching, Mentoring and Organizational Consultancy*. Maidenhead: Open University Press.

*Heron, J. (1993) *Group Facilitation: Theories and Models for Practice*. London: Kogan Page.

Honey, P. and Mumford, A. (1992) *Manual of Learning Styles*. Maidenhead: P. Honey Publications.

*Houston, G. (1990) *The Red Book of Groups*. London: The Rochester Foundation.

Janis, I.L. (1982) *Groupthink*, 2nd edn. Boston, MA: Houghton Mifflin.

Jaques, D. (2000) *Learning in Groups*, 3rd edn. London: Kogan Page.

Karpman, S. (1968) Fairy tales and script drama analysis, *Transactional Analysis Bulletin*, 7(26): 39–43.

Kirkpatrick, D.L. (1996) *Evaluating Training Programmes: The Four Levels*. San Francisco, CA: Berrett-Koehler.

Klein, J. (aka Anonymous) (1996) *Primary Colors: A Novel of Politics*. New York: Random House.

*Kline, N. (1999) *Time To Think*. London: Ward Lock.

Kolb, D.A. (1984) *Experiential Learning*. Englewood Cliffs, NJ: Prentice Hall.

Lencioni, P. (2002) *The Five Dysfunctions of Team*. San Francisco, CA: Jossey-Bass.

Lewin, K. (1948) *Resolving Social Conflicts: Selected Papers on Group Dynamics*. New York: Harper & Row.

*Owen, H. (1997) *Open Space Technology: A User's Guide*. San Francisco, CA: Berrett-Koehler.

Revans, R. (1980) *Action Learning: New Techniques for Management*. London: Blond and Briggs.

Rogers, J. (2007a) *Adults Learning*, 5th edn. Maidenhead: Open University Press.

Rogers, J. (2007b) *Sixteen Personality Types at Work in Organizations*, 2nd edn. London: Management Futures.

*Rosenberg, M.B. (1999) *Nonviolent Communication*. Encinitas, CA: Puddle Dancer Press.

Schein, E.H. (1999) *Process Consultation Revisited: Building the Helping Relationship*. Reading, MA: Addison-Wesley.

Schutz, W. (1958) *FIRO – a Three Dimensional Theory of Interpersonal Behaviour*. New York: Holt, Rheinhart & Wilson.

*Schwartz, R.M. (2002) *The Skilled Facilitator*. San Francisco, CA: Jossey-Bass.

*Senge, P. (1994) *The Fifth Discipline Fieldbook: Strategies for Building a Learning Organization*. London: Nicholas Brealey.

Stewart, I. and Joines, V. (1987, revised 2008) *TA Today: A New Introduction to Transactional Analysis*. Nottingham: Lifespace Publishing.

Sullivan, W. and Rees, J. (2008) *Clean Language: Revealing Metaphors and Opening Minds*. Carmarthen: Crown House Publishing.

Tannenbaum, R. and Schmidt, W.H. (1958) How to choose a leadership pattern, *Harvard Business Review*, 38(2): 95–101.

Tuckman, B.W. (1965) Developmental sequence in small groups, *Psychological Bulletin*, 63: 384–99.

Watkins, J.M. and Mohr, B.J. (2001) *Appreciative Inquiry: Change and the Speed of Imagination*. San Francisco, CA: Jossey-Bass.

*Weaver, R.G. and Farrell, J.D. (1997) *Managers as Facilitators*. San Francisco, CA: Berrett-Koehler.

Weisbord, M. (2004) *Productive Workplaces Revisited*. San Francisco, CA: Jossey-Bass.

*Weisbord, M. and Janoff, S. (2000) *Future Search: An Action Guide to Finding Common Ground in Organizations and Communities*, 2nd edn. San Francisco, CA: Berrett-Koehler.

* These books have a useful focus on the practice of facilitation.

Index

Abilene paradox, groupthink, 39–40
action-learning leaders, leadership, 3
action phase, designing, 97–8
affection, cycles of group life, 43–4,
    46–7
ambiguities
    being liked/being challenging, 180–1
    big issues/bite-size chunks, 178–9
    calm/emotional, 181
    charisma/invisibility, 181–2
    control/standing back, 178
    managing, 177–82
    self-aware/self-obsessed, 179–80
    solutions/chaos, 178
    summary, 183
    wisdom/knowing nothing, 179
analysing, designing, 74–84
appreciative inquiry
    assumptions, 79–80
    designing, 79–81
arguments, 139
Asch experiments, groupthink, 40
assumptions
    appreciative inquiry, 79–80
    facilitation, 21–6
    scenario planning, 77–8
authentic conversations, 24
authority directly challenged, dealing with,
    152–4
authority spectrum, group behaviour, 52

BBC, culture change, 17–18
behaviour see group behaviour; nightmares,
    facilitator; whole group behaviour
being liked/being challenging, ambiguities,
    180–1
big issues/bite-size chunks, ambiguities,
    178–9
Bion, Wilfred, whole group behaviour, 29–30
boss taking over, dealing with, 150–1
boundaries, organizations, 6–7
brainstorming, creativity exercises, 89
budget, practicalities, 106–7

buy-in assessment, decision-making
    techniques, 96–7

calm/emotional, ambiguities, 181
challenge/support matrix, 25–6
challenges to authority, dealing with, 152–4
change
    culture change, 17–18
    facilitation, 22
changing climate, organizations, 6
charisma/invisibility, ambiguities, 181–2
clarifying skills, 122–3
'clean' language, language skills, 125–8
client, establishing the real, 57
client service, venues, 109
coaching professionals, 1
complexity, organizations, 8
conditions, facilitation, 10–11
conference model, large group interventions,
    101
conflict, dealing with, 157–9
consulting cycle
    contracting, 58–61
    feeding back the data, 64
    gaining entry, 57
    gathering data, 61–3
continuum, facilitation as a, 52–3
contracting
    consulting cycle, 58–61
    task clarity, 58–60
    traps, 60–1
control, cycles of group life, 43, 45–6
control/standing back, ambiguities,
    178
conversations, authentic, 24
counter-transference, whole group
    behaviour, 33–4
creativity exercises
    brainstorming, 89
    designing, 89
crises, Kennedy, John F., 138
criteria, creating, decision-making
    techniques, 93–5

culture change, BBC, 17–18
cycles of group life, 42–7
cynicism, dealing with, 140–2

dates, venues, 109
decision-making techniques
    buy-in assessment, 96–7
    criteria, creating, 93–5
    designing, 92–8
    force field analysis, 95–8
    line-out, 95
    voting, 92–3
dependence
    leadership, 30
    whole group behaviour, 30
designing, 64–104
    see also preparation
    action phase, 97–8
    analysing, 74–84
    appreciative inquiry, 79–81
    creativity exercises, 89
    decision-making techniques, 92–8
    games, 90–2
    ground rules, 69–71
    group size, 67–8
    ice-breakers, 71–84
    large group interventions, 98–104
    learning cycle, 65–7
    Myers-Briggs approach, 83–4
    PEST analysis, 74–6
    relationships, improving, 84–8
    scenario planning, 77–9
    stakeholder analysis, 76–7
    'Strawman' discussions, 89–92
    SWOT analysis, 74, 75
    thinking hats approach, 81–2
    time management, 68
    warming up, 69–74
    whys (analytical tool), 82–3
discussion problems, dealing with,
    142–4
drama triangle, transactional analysis (TA),
    35–7
drawing technique, relationships,
    improving, 86–7

early departures, dealing with, 151–2
elephant in the room, organizations, 8–10
environment
    see also PEST analysis
    venues, 108
equipment, venues, 111

evaluating, 164–72
    feedback, 165–71
    objectives, 164–5
    process level, 165
    questions about, 171–2
    reviewing, 171
experiencing, learning cycle, 65–7
external facilitators, vs. internal facilitators,
    13–14

facilitation
    assumptions, 21–6
    change, 22
    conditions, 10–11
    as a continuum, 52–3
    examples, 5
    need for, 5–14
    principles, 21–6
    techniques, 19–21
facilitators
    implications for, 49–53
    internal vs. external, 13–14
    vs. trainers, 11–12
family dynamics, relationships in the group,
    48
feedback
    evaluating, 165–71
    forms, 168–71
    'gallery', 167
    self-development, 175
    session marking, 167–8
    'teabag technique', 169–71
feedback exercise, relationships, improving,
    86
feedback skills, 131–5, 139
    discussion problems, 144
    framing feedback, 132–4
    process review, 134–5
feeding back the data, consulting cycle, 64
fight/flight
    leadership, 31
    whole group behaviour, 31
'fishbowls', relationships, improving, 86
food and drink, venues, 109–11
force field analysis
    decision-making techniques, 95–8
    whole group behaviour, 28–9
Forming phase, cycles of group life, 42
frameworks, group behaviour, 50
framing feedback, feedback skills, 132–4
future search, large group interventions,
    100–1

gaining entry, consulting cycle, 57
'gallery', feedback, 167
games, designing, 90–2
gathering data
    consulting cycle, 61–3
    interviews, 61–2
    observation, 63
    secondary data, 63
ground rules, designing, 69–71
group behaviour
    authority spectrum, 52
    explaining, 49–50
    frameworks, 50
    self-awareness, 50–1
group size, designing, 67–8
group thinking, quality, 28
groupthink, 38–42
    Abilene paradox, 39–40
    Asch experiments, 40
    development, 40–2
    disastrous consequences, 41–2
    mental habits, 41
    Stanford experiment, 40
    symptoms, 38–9

'hamburger model', human process, 14–16
healthcare sector example, drama triangle,
    37
human process
    'hamburger model', 14–16
    importance, 14–21

ice-breakers, designing, 71–84
'in the moment', working, 26
inclusion, cycles of group life, 43, 44–5
informal roles, relationships in the group,
    48–9
internal facilitators, vs. external facilitators,
    13–14
interrupting skills, 121–2
interviews, gathering data, 61–2

Kennedy, John F., crises, 138

language skills, 125–9
    'clean' language, 125–8
    Neuro Linguistic Programming (NLP),
        125
    silence, 128
    specificity, 128, 129
large group interventions
    conference model, 101

designing, 98–104
future search, 100–1
logistics, 104
Open Space approach, 101–4
types, 100–4
late arrivals, dealing with, 151–2
leadership, 27–8
    action-learning leaders, 3
    dependence, 30
    fight/flight, 31
    introduction, 69
    Mandela, Nelson, 116
    skills, 116
learning cycle
    designing, 65–7
    experiencing, 65–7
Lewin, Kurt, whole group behaviour, 28–9
life skill, facilitation as, 3–4
'lighthouse' effect, observing skills, 130
lighting, venues, 107–8
line-out, decision-making techniques, 95
listening skills, 117–20
looking after yourself, self-development,
    175–6
Lord of the Flies, 32

Mandela, Nelson, leadership, 116
marshalling skills, 135–6
matching skills, 123
mechanics skills, 135–7
mediators, 1–2
meeting coordinators, 2–3
mistakes, Smiles, Samuel, 138
Mourning phase, cycles of group life, 43
moving the discussion on, questioning skills,
    124–5
Myers-Briggs approach
    designing, 83–4
    facilitator's tightrope, 177
    problem-solving, 83–4

need for facilitation, 5–14
Neuro Linguistic Programming (NLP), 125
neutrality, 25
nightmares, facilitator, 138–63
    authority directly challenged, 152–4
    boss taking over, 150–1
    conflict, 157–9
    under-contributors, 147–8
    cynicism, 140–2
    discussion problems, 142–4
    early departures, 152–3

late arrivals, 151–2
mobile phones ringing, 162
over-contributors, 149–50
paralysis by analysis, 146–7
principles, 138–40
special needs, 154–7
storming out, 160–2
tangent mania, 144–6
tears, 162–3
whisperers, 159–60
NLP *see* Neuro Linguistic Programming
noise, venues, 108
Norming phase, cycles of group life, 42–3

objectives, evaluating, 164–5
observation, gathering data, 63
observing skills, 129–31
'lighthouse' effect, 130
offending behaviour *see* nightmares,
facilitator
open questions, questioning skills, 124
Open Space approach, large group
interventions, 101–4
organizational consultancy professionals, 1
organizations
boundaries, 6–7
changing climate, 6
complexity, 8
elephant in the room, 8–10
transparency, 7–8
over-contributors, dealing with, 149–51

pairing, whole group behaviour, 31–2
paralysis by analysis, dealing with, 146–7
people needing facilitation, 1–4
perceptions exercise, relationships,
improving, 84–5
Performing phase, cycles of group life,
43
persecutor, drama triangle, 35–7
PEST analysis, designing, 74–6
phones ringing, dealing with, 162
planning *see* preparation
Player, Gary, practise, 164
practicalities, 105–15
achievements, intended, 105
budget, 106–7
venues, 105–15
practise, Player, Gary, 164
preparation, 55–64
see also designing
consulting cycle, 56–64

difficulties, 55–6
planning, 56
principles, facilitation, 21–6
process level, evaluating, 165
process review, feedback skills, 134–5
projection, whole group behaviour, 32–3
prouds/sorries, relationships, improving, 85
psychodynamic approach, whole group
behaviour, 28–32

questioning skills, 124–5
moving the discussion on, 124–5
open questions, 124
questionnaire, self-development, 172–6

recording information skills, 136–7
relationship of equals, 23–4
relationships, improving
designing, 84–8
drawing technique, 86–7
feedback exercise, 86
'fishbowls', 86
perceptions exercise, 84–5
prouds/sorries, 85
well-functioning team, 87–8
relationships in the group, 47–9
family dynamics, 48
informal roles, 48–9
rescuer, drama triangle, 35–7
resourceful clients, 23
reviewing, evaluating, 171
rooms, venues, 111–15
rules, whole group behaviour, 32

scenario planning
assumptions, 77–8
designing, 77–9
seating, venues, 108–9, 112–15
secondary data, gathering data, 63
self-aware/self-obsessed, ambiguities, 179–80
self-awareness, group behaviour, 50–1
self-development, 172–6
feedback, 174–5
looking after yourself, 175–6
questionnaire, 172–4
session marking, feedback, 167–8
signposting skills, 123
silence, language skills, 128
simple/wicked problems, 22–3
skills, 116–37
clarifying, 122–3
feedback, 131–5, 139, 144

interrupting, 121–2
language, 125–9
leadership, 116
listening, 117–20
marshalling, 135–6
matching, 123
mechanics, 135–7
observing, 129–31
questioning, 124–5
recording information, 136–7
signposting, 123
summarizing, 120–1
timekeeping, 135
trust, 116–23
Smiles, Samuel, mistakes, 138
solutions/chaos, ambiguities, 178
special needs, dealing with, 154–7
specificity, language skills, 128, 129
stakeholder analysis, designing, 76–7
Stanford experiment, groupthink, 40
storming out, dealing with, 160–2
Storming phase, cycles of group life,
    42
'Strawman' discussions, designing,
    89–92
summarizing skills, 120–1
summary, ambiguities, 182–3
support/challenge matrix, 25–6
SWOT analysis, designing, 74, 75

TA *see* transactional analysis
tangent mania, dealing with, 144–6
task clarity, contracting, 58–60
'teabag technique', feedback, 169–71
teachers, 2
team coaching professionals, 1
tears, dealing with, 162–3
thinking, group *see* group thinking;
    groupthink
thinking hats approach, designing, 81–2
tightrope, facilitator's, 176–8
time management, designing, 68
timekeeping skills, 135
trainers, 2
    vs. facilitators, 11–12
transactional analysis (TA)
    drama triangle, 35–7
    whole group behaviour, 34–7
transference, whole group behaviour, 33–4
transparency, organizations, 7–8

trust skills, 116–23
    clarifying, 122–3
    interrupting, 121–2
    listening skills, 117–20
    matching, 123
    signposting, 123
    summarizing, 120–1

under-contributors, dealing with, 147–8

venues
    client service, 109
    dates, 109
    environment, 108
    equipment, 111
    food and drink, 109–11
    lighting, 107–8
    noise, 108
    practicalities, 105–15
    rooms, 111–15
    seating, 108–9, 112–15
victim, drama triangle, 35–7
voting, decision-making techniques,
    92–3

warming up, designing, 69–74
well-functioning team, relationships,
    improving, 87–8
whisperers, dealing with, 159–60
whole group behaviour, 28–37
    Bion, Wilfred, 29–30
    counter-transference, 33–4
    dependence, 30
    fight/flight, 31
    force field analysis, 28–9
    Lewin, Kurt, 28–9
    pairing, 31–2
    projection, 32–3
    psychodynamic approach, 28–32
    rules, 32
    transactional analysis (TA), 34–7
    transference, 33–4
    Young, Robert M., 29–30
whys (analytical tool), designing, 82–3
wicked/simple problems, 22–3
wisdom/knowing nothing, ambiguities, 179
working 'in the moment', 26

Young, Robert M.
    whole group behaviour, 29–30